CREATIVE KNITTING

CREATIVE KNITTING

(You'll never need another pattern!)

Sherry Wilson

DAVID & CHARLES

Newton Abbot   London

ISBN 0 7153 7982 8

First published in New Zealand by A. H. & A. W. Reed Ltd,
Wellington, New Zealand.

This edition first published in the United Kingdom in 1980 by
David & Charles (Publishers) Ltd, Newton Abbot, Devon
Printed by Kyodo-Shing Loong Printing Industries Pte Ltd, Singapore.

CONTENTS

To fellow knitters, everywhere.

INTRODUCTION

Handknitting — fascinating, therapeutic and satisfying — is one of the most creative and international of handcrafts. This is a craft which will never die out.

This book presents a full range of basic knitting patterns in all sizes which can be used to create original versions of any garment. It opens the way to new and exciting ideas and creative possibilities. The choice of style and the stitch pattern you knit will be yours. Every garment you produce will reflect your mark of individuality and you will have created it. It shows you how to create your own patterns of various stitches and styles of Fair Isle (you don't have to be able to draw) and for those who have not yet attempted Aran knitting, it includes a full, step-by-step familiarisation course.

The garments illustrated in the photographs are my own versions, but should you wish to copy any of them, details are given. Do not be afraid to tackle something you think may be beyond you. If you can do a knit stitch and a purl stitch you can do *any* pattern, because knit and purl are all there is to knitting.

Please read right through the front sections of this book before you commence any garment. There are many hints which you might like to put into practice.

Happy knitting!

(Sherry Wilson)

1. Getting started

Purchasing wool

Before making any garment it is most important to ensure that sufficient wool is available from the same dye-lot to complete the chosen pattern. To avoid disappointment, over-order a little unless the wool shop is prepared to keep some aside. One extra ball should always be allowed if crepe wool is substituted for standard wool specified in the pattern.

Some problems may be encountered in purchasing wool in metric quantities for use in an older pattern with English measurements. One ounce is equivalent to 28.35 grams, but for this purpose can be considered as just over half a 50-gram ball. Two 25-gram balls or one 50-gram ball would therefore be required to complete a pattern requiring one ounce of wool. The following chart provides a quick reference for converting English to metric quantities and vice versa.

You will require

	25-gram balls	50-gram balls
1 ounce (28.35 grams)	2	1
2 ounces (56.70 grams)	3	2
3 ounces (85.05 grams)	4	2
4 ounces (113.40 grams)	5	3
5 ounces (141.80 grams)	6	3
6 ounces (170.10 grams)	7	4
7 ounces (198.40 grams)	8	4
8 ounces (226.80 grams)	10	5
9 ounces (255.10 grams)	11	6
10 ounces (283.50 grams)	12	6
11 ounces (311.80 grams)	13	7
12 ounces (340.20 grams)	14	7
13 ounces (368.50 grams)	15	8
14 ounces (396.90 grams)	16	8
15 ounces (425.20 grams)	18	9
16 ounces (453.60 grams)	19	10
17 ounces (481.95 grams)	20	10
18 ounces (510.30 grams)	21	11
19 ounces (538.65 grams)	22	11
20 ounces (567.00 grams)	23	12
21 ounces (595.35 grams)	24	12
22 ounces (623.70 grams)	25	13
23 ounces (625.05 grams)	27	14
24 ounces (680.40 grams)	28	14
25 ounces (708.75 grams)	29	15
26 ounces (737.00 grams)	30	15
27 ounces (765.35 grams)	31	16
28 ounces (793.70 grams)	32	16
29 ounces (822.05 grams)	33	17
30 ounces (850.40 grams)	35	18

Size variants

During the researching of this book, three children were discovered with 56 cm (22 in.) chests. They were a plump little baby of nine months, a boy of three years and a slender schoolboy of seven years. As similar garments would obviously be unsuitable for such wide age ranges, a considerable amount of freedom has been allowed in the structuring of the basic patterns. There has been no attempt to classify certain chest sizes as suitable for babywear or toddlers' wear; rather, the reader is encouraged to match the pattern to the age of the recipient and select the suitable chest size.

Tension

Purchasing the wool specified in a knitting pattern and using the needle sizes stated does not guarantee that the resulting garment will be the correct size and fitting. Individual differences in knitting style can produce widely-varying samples which are compounded in a finished garment. Different brands of wool vary in thickness and double-knitting wool alone has been found to range from a normal 4-ply weight to almost a triple knit. For these reasons the importance of checking your tension cannot be overstressed. It takes very little time to knit a small sample square and the results are invariably worthwhile.

Using the appropriate needles (3¼ mm for 4-ply and 4 mm for double-knitting), cast on 18 or 20 stitches and knit 20 rows in stocking stitch. Pin out and press the work, turn and pin down the corners and sides. Check that the tension corresponds to that on the accompanying diagrams. If the sample square has a smaller number of stitches per centimetre, use larger needles. If a greater number, smaller needles should be used. (Even half a stitch in variation will affect the size of the finished work, and this should be taken into account when assessing the tension.)

Double-knitting

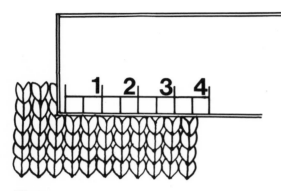

5½ sts.
    = 2.5 cm (1 in.)
7½ rows

11 sts.
    = 5 cm (2 in.)
15 rows

4-ply

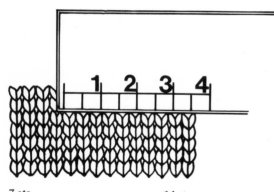

7 sts.
    = 2.5 cm (1 in.)
9 rows

14 sts.
    = 5 cm (2 in.)
18 rows

Needle conversions

Metric size		English size	
	8 mm		0
	7½ mm		1
	7 mm		2
	6½ mm		3
	6 mm		4
	5½ mm		5
	5 mm		6
	4½ mm		7
	4 mm		8
	3¾ mm		9
	3¼ mm		10
	3 mm		11
	2¾ mm		12
	2¼ mm		13
	2 mm		14

Abbreviations

Abbreviations used throughout this book are as follows:

Alt.	Alternate
Beg.	Beginning
Cm	Centimetre(s)
Comm.	Commence
Cont.	Continue
Dec.	Decrease
Foll.	Following
In.	Inch(es)
Inc.	Increase
K.	Knit
P.	Purl
P.s.s.o.	Pass slipped stitch over
Rem.	Remain
Rept.	Repeat
R.s.f.	Right side facing
Sl. 1	Slip next stitch without knitting it
St(s).	Stitch(es)
Stst.	Stocking stitch
T.b.l.	Through back of loops
Tog.	Together
Wl. fwd.	Wool forward
Wl. fwd. (twice)	Wind wool 1½ times around needle
W.s.f.	Wrong side facing

2. Knitting know-how

Casting on

There are many methods of casting on, but the one which the author has found to be the best is detailed below. This method, while giving a firm cast-on row, also seems to have a little more elasticity than other methods and bands of ribbing done this way are less likely to stretch out of shape as the garment gets older.

1. Knot the wool around the two needles, which should be placed side by side.
2. Knit the first stitch, pull the loop through and place on the left-hand needle.

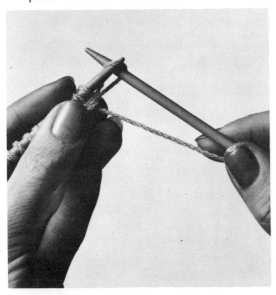

3. *Remove the right-hand needle and insert it behind both sides of the previous stitch.
4. Put the wool around the needle, pull the loop through, place it on the left-hand needle and repeat from *.

Casting off ribbing

This should always be done ribwise, using needles one size larger, unless you are an extremely loose knitter. (Ribwise: knit or purl the appropriate stitches, according to the previous row, as they are cast off. This keeps the final row "elastic".)

Slipping the first stitch

It is advisable to slip the first stitch of every row. This results in eliminating some of the curl of the knitting and saving a certain amount of wool.

On a purl row, slip the first stitch knitwise. Remember, however, that if a pattern is being worked, this first slipped stitch corresponds to stitch "1" of the instructions.

Measuring sleeves

When knitting a sleeve, always measure the under-arm length along the side of the knitting, not straight up from commencement, as this measurement will vary almost 2 mm in every 2.5. cm. It is the sides of the knitted sleeve which will become the underarm seam, and therefore this is the part which should be measured.

Correcting mistakes

If a mistake has been made within the last two rows, it is worthwhile unpicking the work stitch by stitch to reach it. If it has occurred further down the work, however, pull the needle right out and unravel the knitting until the mistake has been eliminated and the end of a row has been reached. Then, using a needle two sizes smaller, pick up the stitches. Ideally, the used, crinkled wool should be broken off and discarded and fresh wool tied in at the beginning of the row. If a large amount of wool has been unravelled, wind this around a book, tray or chair-back, tie it loosely with a contrast thread in two places, wash, and hang in the shade to dry. This can be rewound and used later.

After picking up the stitches it will probably be found that many have reversed their position on the needle. Knit or purl (as the case may be) into the backs of these stitches and they will automatically be righted.

Joining wool and finishing

When commencing a new ball of wool, always join it in at the armhole edge of the work. Break off any lengths of wool not quite long enough to complete the next row and keep these lengths for sewing up the garment. Weave the two ends along the row for three or four stitches or darn them all into the side seams before stitching up the garment. Snip off any protruding loose ends. If these have been woven along for several stitches they will be firmly held and will never unravel. (See Fair Isle section on weaving in.)

Sewing up

Place the edges right sides together, and pin in a few places to hold the work and to prevent it from stretching. Anchor one end of the seam with two or three overstitches and sew using the backstitch method. The seam should be made just below the cast-off edges or just in from the side seam edges. A tapestry needle is ideal for this purpose as it is shorter and blunter than a darning needle and has a larger eye, making threading easier. Join the ribbed sections using an overstitch.

Pressing

The floor is often preferable to an ironing board for pressing the pieces of a newly-knitted garment. Spread out two large towels or a doubled blanket on the carpet or a mat near an electric point. This provides ample space so the sections can be easily matched and pinned out to their correct measurements. Press each piece on the wrong side with a steam iron over a cloth, or a fairly-hot, dry iron over a dampened cloth. Do not press the ribbing.

Pressing seams (this can be done on the ironing board): After sewing up the garment, turn it inside out and press the seams. In the case of awkward little pieces (such as a baby's bootee or a knitted toy) stuff

with an old nylon stocking or a man's handkerchief. The article can then be rolled around while the seam is pressed.

Pressing sleeve seams: Turn the garment inside out. If it is a baby's garment, lie the sleeve flat with the seam upwards in the centre of the sleeve. Fold a tea towel and slip it down inside the sleeve. Press the seam. For an adult's garment, wrap a tea towel around a rolling pin, slide it down inside the sleeve and press the seam, moving the bolster as required. These methods eliminate possible unsightly marks on the right side of the sleeve when the seam is pressed with nothing sandwiched in between.

Ribbed bands

Select the required ribbing pattern but remember that with a cardigan or button-to-the-neck style, the front borders must be worked in the same stitch as the bands.

The most frequently-used type of ribbing is the k.1, p.1 rib. The 2 × 2 rib (k.2, p.2) is also popular. The following variations are suited to a male garment in the first instance, while the second is a more feminine stitch.

1. *Fisherman's rib.* (K.1, p.1) for the 1st row, but in every k.st. thereafter, the r.h. needle should be pushed through the base of the st. on the previous row, then knitted and slipped off the l.h. needle as usual.

This gives a chunkier 1 × 1 rib than the finer, common 1 × 1 rib.

2. *Twist 2 rib.* P.2, (k. into the back of the 2nd st. on the l.h. needle then into the front of the 1st st., slipping both off the needle tog., p.2). On the 2nd row, k. the 2 p. sts. from the previous row and p. the 2 k. sts. at the back of the twist.

This stitch looks delightful on a garment where the main body is in plain stocking stitch (see page 14).

A moss stitch band is pretty, but it will not hold the garment quite as firmly around the wrist, waist or hip as a ribbed band.

It is preferable, for the sake of balance, to work the front and back bands, cuffs and neck edging in the same ribbed stitch.

Sewing on buttons

Lie the finished garment on a smooth surface. Match up the front sections so that the lower edges are together with the buttonholed front overlapping the other. Pin at the base to hold firm. Then, with small, gold safety-pins, reach through each buttonhole, pick up two stitches and fasten the safety-pins up to the neck edge. Slip the buttonholes over all the safety-pins, leaving the pins in place as button markers. Use shirring elastic to sew buttons onto garments for lively children. If pulled or caught during play the buttons will then spring back into place, reducing the risk of tearing the front border of the garment.

Front borders
(For v-necked and high-necked cardigans)

The front borders can be knitted with the front sections, or they can be worked separately. If the second method is used, place the required number of stitches on a safety-pin after knitting the bands. These stitches can then be picked up later and knitted on smaller-sized needles.

The author's preference is to knit the borders with the front sections, as this eliminates the need for a seam. One advantage of using the second method, however, is that the borders can be worked on finer needles to match the bands. Working on the borders alone also gives a better opportunity to concentrate on the spacing of buttonholes.

In the basic pattern instructions the borders are included with the front sections but if the second method is preferred, simply disregard "Rib 6 sts." in the instructions and continue with the instructions for the main body of the front sections.

If a wider border is desired this may be increased by up to three stitches on each side without appreciably altering the size of the garment. Remember, however, to take the extra stitches into account when following the pattern instructions.

It is very easy to confuse the fronts of cardigans or lumberjacket styles and to find, to your horror, you have knitted two left or two right fronts. When working the fronts remember that for the left front, every r.s.f. row should be commenced at the armhole edge. For the right front, every r.s.f. row should be commenced at the ribbed front border.

When graphing a pattern for an open-fronted garment, it is necessary to make a distinction between the last border stitch and the main pattern. This should take the form of a contrast stitch at the inside edge of each front border; a purl stitch next to stocking stitch or a knit stitch next to reversed stocking stitch.

Example — setting of border stitches beside stocking stitch panel:

Right front		Left front
6 5 4 3 2 1	r.s.f.	1 2 3 4 5 6
P.k.p.k.p.k. (slip)		(slip) K.p.k.p.k.p.

The right-front pattern (commencing at each r.s.f. row at front border) for this garment will read:
1st row: Sl.1 knitwise, p.1, k.1, p.1, k.1, p.1, k. to end.
2nd row: (w.s.f.) Sl.1, p. (or pattern) to last 6 sts., k.1, p.1, k.1, p.1, k.1, p.1.

The left-front pattern (commencing every r.s.f. row at armhole edge) will read:

1st row: Sl.1, k. to last 6 sts., p.1, k.1, p.1, k.1, p.1, k.1.
2nd row: (w.s.f.) Sl.1 knitwise, k.1, p.1, k.1, p.1, k.1, p. to end.

If, on completion of a band, it is found that the border stitches have been miscalculated, turn the work to check whether a further row will correct the error and purl one row on 3¼ mm needles. This will not show on the right side of the work and the pattern can then be commenced.

If bands and front borders are to be worked in a 2 × 2 rib, the right-front pattern, after completion of the band, will read:

1st row: (r.s.f.) Sl.1, p.1, k.2, p.2, k. (or pattern) to end.
2nd row: (w.s.f.) Sl.1, p. to last 6 sts., k.2, p.2, k.2.

The left-front pattern will read:

1st row: (r.s.f.) Sl.1, k. (or pattern) to last 6 sts., p.2, k.2, p.2.
2nd row: (w.s.f.) Sl.1, k.1, p.2, k.2, p. (or pattern) to end.

Right front   Left front

6 5 4 3 2 1   R.S.F.   1 2 3 4 5 6

P.p.k.k.p.p. (slip)   (slip) P.p.k.k.p.p.

Buttonholes

When making a cardigan or button-to-the-neck garment, it is advisable to complete the front without buttonholes first. The number of buttonholes in the opposite front can then be calculated, beginning from the third to fourth rows from the lower edge of the band.

V-necked cardigans: Buttonholes cease when the armhole is reached and the front shapings begin.

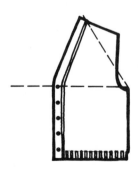

Mark the top and lower buttonholes and calculate the number required in between. A distance of approximately 5 cm (2 in.) between buttonholes is ideal.

High-necked cardigans: If the garment has a round neckband, the top buttonhole must be calculated to fall in the centre (third to fourth rows) of the neckband. If a collar is required, however, the top buttonhole should fall between the second and third rows from the top of the front border (see illustrations).

 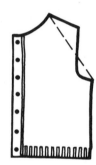

Raglan shapings

Before the pieces of a raglan-shaped garment are pressed, the raglan shapings should be stretched between the hands. This will "seat" the decreasings.

To obtain neat raglan shapings, regardless of stitch pattern, work as follows:

r.s.f.: K.2, k.2 tog., pattern to last 4 sts., k.2 tog. t.b.l., k.2.
w.s.f.: P.3, pattern to last 3 sts., p.3.

Simplifying pattern instructions

The directions in this book have been reduced to basics to provide a clear and easy-to-follow text.

Row-by-row instructions for ribbed bands have been simplified to "Rib x rows" (except where the setting of the stitches is vital to the pattern). A problem which frequently occurs is in the counting of the stitch remaining on the right-hand needle after several stitches have been cast off. This stitch is not included in the patterns in this book and an instruction reading "Cast off 3 sts., k.7" will have 8 stitches remaining on the right-hand needle.

Note: Unless otherwise stated, always end any section of instructions with a purl (or wrong side) row.

Hints

How to obtain a neat stripe in a ribbed band

Work as follows:

w.s.f.: Join in contrast colour. P.1 row. Rib next rows for width of stripe desired.

r.s.f.: Rejoin main colour, k.1 row, then continue in rib.

Troubleshooting

When resuming knitting after an interruption or a pause, scrutinise the work carefully. Errors can then be corrected easily.

Drying garments

Never dry pale-coloured wool in the sun. White wool will discolour and pinks, blues and other pastel colours will fade.

Identification of garments

Children's schoolwear can be made easily identifiable by the addition of an unusual mark. Embroider the initials inside the cuff or neckband, or stitch a contrasting thread inside the back neckband. A tassel of contrasting thread could also be attached to the shoulder seam.

A tab of contrasting thread stitched inside at the back neck of a jersey will enable small children to distinguish the back from the front.

Unisex

If a garment is suitable for a boy or a girl, work buttonholes in both front borders, sewing the buttons over the appropriate holes. If the garment is passed on, the buttons can be resewn on to the opposite front and there will still be a set of corresponding buttonholes.

When leaving the work

Always finish a row of knitting to avoid stretching the last stitch.

To avoid tangles

Always use wool from the inside of the ball unless otherwise stated on the label. Knitting from the wrong end of the ball puts a reverse twist on the thread and causes tangles.

Plate 1

Plate 2

Plate 3

Plate 4

Plate 5

Plate 6

Plate 7

Plate 8

Plate 9

3. Choosing a pattern

Graphing a pattern

It is advisable, before commencing any garment, to spend some time drawing a correctly-centred pattern. It is especially important that fancy panels are equidistant and meet on the shoulders to achieve a professional look.

For this purpose a supply of graph paper is essential. Each square represents one stitch, and the heavier line occurring each block of ten squares makes stitch counting easier. If working a recurring pattern of a Fair Isle motif it is only necessary to graph the number of rows required to "set" the pattern or "cover" the motif. When working a motif from a graph, the knit rows should be read from right to left and the purl rows from left to right.

A stationer or stamp dealer will sell graph paper in loose sheets. These will have to be cut and joined when graphing larger sizes. Overlap and glue the pages or carefully sellotape the back of the join. When graphing a pattern with an uneven number of stitches, there will be a single centre stitch. When graphing a pattern with an even number of stitches, however, there will be a centre line which will fall between two stitches.

To graph a pattern

1. Check the basic pattern in the size required.
2. Mark out the number of stitches required on the graph paper.
3. Decide on the stitch pattern.

Any stitch pattern must be centred to avoid giving the garment a lopsided appearance. For instance, a 4 x 1 rib pattern (4k. 1p.) must be similar at each side of the knitting, regardless of the number of knit and purl stitches appearing at each end.

Read through the following example: 57 stitches worked in 4 x 1 rib.

1. Mark out 57 stitches on the graph and experiment until the pattern is centred. It could appear something like this:

Key: / equals knit stitches
    X equals purl stitches   xx////x////x////x////x////x////x////x////x////x////xx

2. With the right side facing, this pattern would read: Sl.1, p.1, (k.4, p.1) to last st., p.1.

When working two front pieces, it is important that the pattern begins correctly just inside the ribbed borders (when knitting a cardigan of any kind)

Example: a front of 36 stitches worked in 4 x 1 rib: (Key: 0 equals border stitches)

1. *Left front:* ////X////X////X////X////X////X000000
2. With the right side facing this pattern would read: Sl.1, k.3, (p.1, k.4) to last 7 sts., p.1, work border sts.
3. *Right front:* 000000X////X////X////X////X////X////
4. With the right side facing, this pattern would read:
   Work 6 border sts., (p.1, k.4) to end.

If a stitch is being added or subtracted from each side of an open-fronted garment, adjust the back pattern accordingly by adding or subtracting one stitch from the total.

Graphing a central-patterned panel

1. Decide upon the stitch width of the panel.
2. If the pattern stipulates an even number of stitches, an even number will be required for the panel.
3. If the stitch is uneven, an uneven number of stitches must be used in the panel.

It is possible, however, to add or subtract one stitch from the basic instructions to fit a chosen stitch pattern or a special panel. This stitch must be taken into consideration throughout the knitting of the garment piece. If a stitch is being added or subtracted from each side of an open-fronted garment, adjust the back pattern accordingly by adding or subtracting one stitch from the total. (If an even number of stitches is being used for a v-necked jumper, the centre stitch must be "made" when dividing for the "V" by picking up the loop from the row below and marking this as the centre stitch.)

Example: (A) Graphing a central panel, 78 stitches required for the correct fit.

1. Mark 78 stitches on the graph.

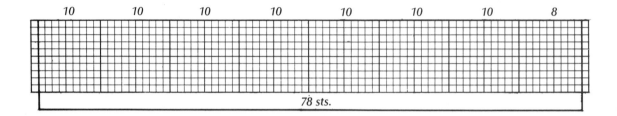

A central panel 20 stitches wide corresponds to the total stitch number of 78 (both are even numbers).

2. To find the centre of the garment piece, divide 78 by 2. This gives 39 stitches on either side of a centre line.

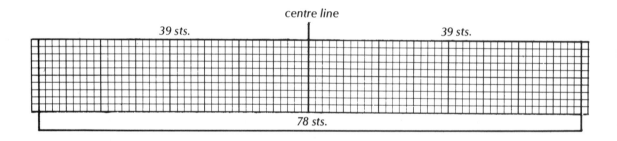

If the centre line of the panel (with 10 stitches on either side) is placed over the centre line of the complete piece, it can be seen that the panel occupies 10 stitches out of 39 on each side of the centre line.

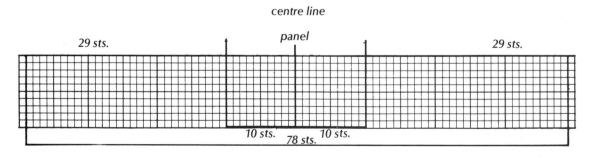

3. Graph the panel stitches.

Example: a panel with a twist-2 cable on either side. Mark 2 panel stitches on either side of the graph. This occupies 4 out of 20 panel stitches. In order to keep the twist-2 in maximum relief, it would be advisable to insert a number of purl stitches beside it. In this case, mark 3 purl stitches on the inside of each twist-2 cable. There are now 10 panel stitches remaining. The remaining space in this example has a basket-weave section. Mark the k.2, p.2 stitches across the 10 centre squares then mark the next (purl) row as it will appear from the front. On the third row of this section, those stitches previously knitted are purled and vice versa, to form the basket-weave pattern.

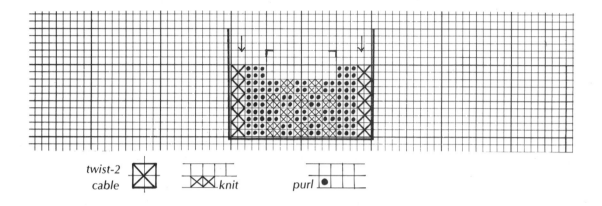

twist-2 cable ▧   ▨ knit   purl ▣

If the main body of the garment is to be worked in stocking stitch, the pattern will read as follows:
1st row: K.29, tw.2, p.3, k.2, (p.2, k.2) twice, p.3, tw.2, k.29.
2nd row: P.31 (p. the 2 sts. on reverse side of the tw.2), k.3, p.2, (k.2, p.2) twice, k.3, p.31.
3rd row: K.29, tw.2, p.5, k.2, p.2, k.2, p.5, tw.2, k.29.
4th row: P.31, k.5, p.2, k.2, p.2, k.5, p.31.

These four rows complete one pattern and must be repeated for the length required. To "set" the pattern, it is necessary to graph only the number of rows required for one pattern section.

Example: (B)

Where a pattern specifies an uneven number of overall stitches and an uneven number of panel stitches, there will be a remaining centre stitch. If 79 stitches are required, a 21 stitch centre panel would be appropriate (both are uneven numbers).
1. Mark 79 stitches on the graph.
2. To find the centre stitch divide 79 by 2. This gives 39 plus 1, indicating that the 40th stitch counted from either end is the centre stitch. If the centre stitch of the panel (with 10 stitches on either side) is placed over the centre stitch of the complete piece, it can be seen that the panel occupies 10 stitches out of 39 on each side of the centre stitch.

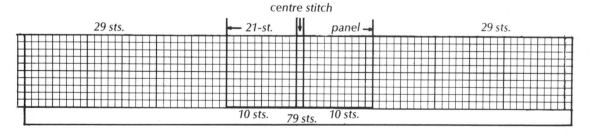

29 sts.   centre stitch   21-st.   panel →   29 sts.

10 sts.   79 sts.   10 sts.

11

Graphing patterned side panels

If a patterned panel is desired on each side of the centre front, the placing is as follows (two 21-stitch panels over 78 stitches):

1. Find the centre line of the main piece by dividing 78 by 2. This gives 39 stitches on each side.
2. Find the centre stitch (as 39 is an uneven number) of each side by dividing 39 by 2. This gives 19 plus 1, indicating that the 20th stitch is the centre stitch of each side.
3. Find the centre stitch of the 21-stitch panel, and place this over the centre stitch of each side.

It can be seen that the 21-stitch panel occurs after 9 side stitches and is followed by 18 central stitches (9 plus 9), the second 21-stitch panel and another 9 side stitches.

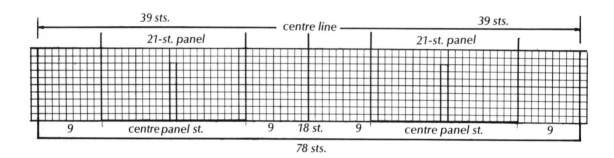

A central panel or two patterned side panels can be effectively combined with matching sleeve panels.

Marker threads: Use two short lengths of contrasting wool to mark each side of a panel. Simply lay the thread across work between 2 stitches, and flip it across each row as you knit up to it. When the panel has become fully established and the work has reached the length where you can see at a glance where the panel starts and finishes, remove the threads.

A selection of stitch patterns

Basket-weave

1st row: (K.2, p.2) to end.
2nd row: (P.2, k.2) to end.
3rd row: (P.2, k.2) to end.
4th row: (K.2, p.2) to end.
4 rows = 1 pattern. 34 sts. used.

An old favourite, this pattern is better left unpressed.

"Bluebell"

1st row: (P.3, k.3) to last 3 sts., p.3.
2nd row: (K.3, p.3) to last 3 sts., k.3.
3rd row: (P.3, sl.1, k.2 tog., p.s.s.o.) to last 3 sts., p.3.
4th row: (K.3, p. into lower loop between next 2 sts., p.1, p. into lower loop) to last 3 sts., k.3.
4 rows = 1 pattern. 33 sts. used.

An attractive stitch for all-over use, or for a panel.

Moss and lace panels

1st row: P.1, k.5, p.1, *(k.1, p.1) 4 times, k.5, p.1. Rept. from * to end.
2nd row: K.1, p.5, k.1, *(k.1, p.1) 3 times, k.2, p.5, k.1. Rept. from * to end.
3rd row: P.1, k.2 tog., wl. fwd., k.1, wl. fwd., sl.1, k.1, p.s.s.o., p.1, *(k.1, p.1) 4 times, k.2 tog., wl. fwd., k.1, wl. fwd., sl.1, k.1, p.s.s.o., p.1. Rept. from * to end.
4th row: As 2nd row.
4 rows = 1 pattern. 35 sts. used.

An attractive "body" stitch, when contrasted with stocking stitch sleeves.

Twist-2 rib

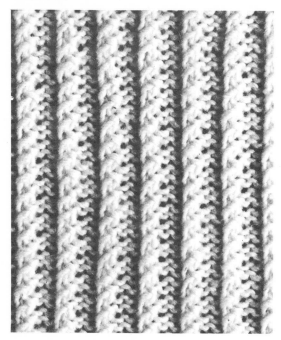

1st row: (P.2, k. twice into next st.) to end.
2nd row: (P.2 tog., k.2) to end.
2 rows = 1 pattern. 33 sts. used.
   An ideal "skinny-rib" stitch, suited to all ages.

"Knobby" rib

1st row: (P.2, k.1, t.b.l.) to end.
2nd row: K.
2 rows = 1 pattern. 33 sts. used.
   A good all-over stitch, also suited to all ages.

"Loop" rib

1st row: (K.1, make 1 by knitting loop from previous row, k.2 tog.) to end.
2nd row: (K.1, wl. fwd., k.2 tog.) to end.
3rd row: K.
4th row: P.
4 rows = 1 pattern. 33 sts. used.
   An unusual but attractive all-over stitch giving a semi-lacy effect.

Versatile broken rib

1st row: (K.1, p.2) to end.
2nd row: (K.2, p.1) to end.
3rd row: K.
4th row: P.
4 rows = 1 pattern. 33 sts. used.
   A versatile stitch, suited to all ages.

Cross-2 rib

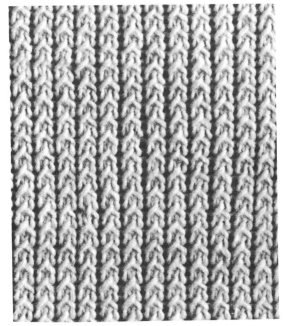

(Cross 2: K. into front of 2nd st. on l.h. needle, lift over 1st. st. and slip off, then k. into front of 1st. st.)

1st row: (Cross 2) to end.
2nd row: P.

2 rows = 1 pattern. 34 sts. used.

This is an ideal panel stitch, but it is not suitable for an all-over stitch as it is too firm.

Lace pattern

1st row: K.1, wl. fwd., sl.1, k.1, p.s.s.o., k.1, *k.1, k.2 tog., wl. fwd. twice (wool round needle 1½ times), sl.1, k.1, p.s.s.o., k.1. Rept. from * to last 5 sts., k.1, k.2 tog., wl. fwd., k.2.
2nd row: P.5, *p.2, (p.1, k.1 into long st.), p.2. Rept. from * to last 4 sts., p.4.
3rd row: K.2, wl. fwd., sl.1, k.1, p.s.s.o., *k.2 tog., wl. fwd., k.2, wl. fwd., sl.1, k.1, p.s.s.o. Rept. from * to last 5 sts., k.2 tog., wl. fwd., k.3.
4th row: P.
5th row: K.3, k.2 tog., wl. fwd., *wl. fwd., sl.1, k.1, p.s.s.o., k.2, k.2 tog., wl. fwd. Rept. from * to last 4 sts., wl. fwd., sl.1, k.1, p.s.s.o., k.2.
6th row: P.3, (p.1, k.1) into long st., *p.4, (p.1, k.1) into long st. Rept. from * to last 4 sts., p.4.
7th row: K.2, k.2 tog., wl. fwd., k.1, *k.1, wl. fwd., sl.1, k.1, p.s.s.o., k.2 tog., wl. fwd., k.1. Rept. from * to last 4 sts., k.1, wl. fwd., sl.1, k.1, p.s.s.o., k.1.
8th row: P.

8 rows = 1 pattern. 33 sts. used.

An exquisite lace pattern for babywear or ladies' fashion garments.

Broken rib

1st row: (P.2, k.2) to end.
2nd row: (K.2, p.2) to end.
3rd row: (r.s.f.) p.
4th row: P.

4 rows = 1 pattern. 34 sts. used.

A useful stitch for any jumper or cardigan.

Diagonal rib

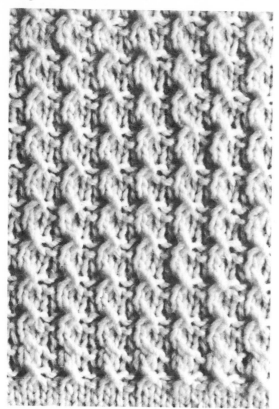

"Chunky" broken rib

1st row: K.

2nd row: P.

3rd row: P.1, (k. into back of 2nd st. on l.h. needle, then into front of 1st st., slipping both off together, p.1) to end.

4th row: K.1, (p. into front of 2nd st. on l.h. needle, then p. into front of 1st st., slipping both off together, k.1) to end.

4 rows = 1 pattern. 34 sts. used.

   An attractive stitch suited to all age groups.

1st row: K.

2nd row: K.1, (p.2, k.1) to end.

3rd row: As 2nd row.

4th row: K.1, (k.2, p.1) to last 3 sts., k.3.

4 rows = 1 pattern. 34 sts. used.

   Ideal for all ages and all garments.

Fair Isle

The back of any Fair Isle work should look as neat as the front. This is achieved by weaving in the unused loops of wool which might otherwise catch on fingers or jewellery. With this method, the wool not in use is woven over and under the working strand until it is required. This involves holding up the strand of wool not in use (referred to hereafter as the "trailing colour") as the stitches below it are knitted with the working colour, and then holding it down while the next stitches are knitted above it.

Trailing strand in down position

hand-held colour. When "hooking" stitches this way on a purl row, it will be found on the next knit row, that the "hooked" stitches are reversed on the left-hand needle. Simply knit into the backs of these stitches to right them automatically.

Trailing strand in up position

Before commencing a row of Fair Isle, glance along the instructions to determine which is the dominant colour. This shade should become the "knitting" strand and the remaining colour(s) "trailing" strand(s). If there are three stitches or less of the trailing colour in any group, these can be "knitted" by hooking the required strand through the stitch with the right-hand needle; rather similar to crocheting. This eliminates the continual need to change the

"Hooking" a stitch

17

Each person develops an individual style of holding the wool for this purpose and it is important only to ensure that the trailing strand flows freely across the back of the work. If this method has not previously been attempted it would be advisable to practise with spare pieces of wool. The following checkerboard pattern uses two colours. One should be light (L) and the other dark (D).

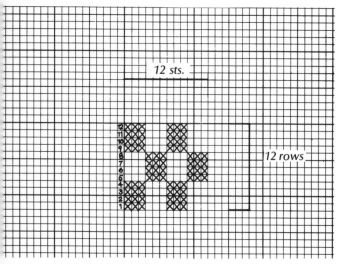

12 sts.

12 rows

(When interpreting a Fair Isle chart, the knit rows should be read from right to left on the graph and the purl rows from left to right.) The pattern for the checkerboard Fair Isle will therefore read:
Cast on 12 sts.
1st row: K.3L, 3D, 3L, 3D.
2nd row: P.3D, 3L, 3D, 3L.
Rept. each row once.
5th row: K.3D, 3L, 3D, 3L.
6th row: P.3L, 3D, 3L, 3D.
Rept. the last two rows once.

As this pattern has an equal number of light and dark stitches, it should not be necessary to change the hand-held colour. Instead, knit the three dark stitches and "hook" the three light ones. On the next knit row reverse the order and knit the three light stitches and "hook" the three dark ones. This ensures that the same stitches are not constantly "'hooked" and will not retreat into the knitting.

When commencing a new ball of wool or starting a new colour (where the Fair Isle pattern is an over-all one) join the wool in at the beginning of a row. Weave the two short ends along for three or four stitches and cut them off. They will be firmly held if woven in properly and a large amount of time, which would otherwise be spent darning in ends, is saved.

If a central or two side motifs are to be worked in

Fair Isle, join in the motif colour two stitches before the beginning of the Fair Isle (use two balls of the motif colour if working two side motifs). Weave for two stitches past the end of motif, dropping the motif colour and working to end of row in the main colour. The side of each panel should be marked at this stage, as outlined at the end of the section on graphing a pattern.

Graphing Fair Isle

(Read the instructions on graphing a panel first.)

Virtually any design can be worked in Fair Isle but some designs lend themselves more favourably to this purpose than others. An equal number of stitches and rows does not produce a square, in fact there are more rows to the centimetre than there are stitches. This is demonstrated by the tension of the basic patterns in this book, which is worked as 11 stitches and 15 rows to 5 centimetres (or $5\frac{1}{2}$ stitches and $7\frac{1}{2}$ rows to the inch). Although any drawing can be traced onto a graph, remember that the design, whilst appearing in proportion on the graph, will, in fact, be somewhat flattened in its final knitted state. For this reason it is well to accentuate the depth of any motif, especially animal or bird designs.

The following bird design is a good example:

Draw the bird to the size required and trace on to graph paper, ignoring the legs, beak and eye (these can be embroidered on later).

Now draw around the graph squares close to the outline, but accentuate the bird's plumpness by graphing beyond the upper and lower curves. The

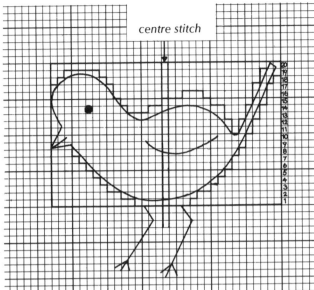

centre stitch

resulting "squared-off" drawing may not resemble the original bird, but when knitted as a Fair Isle motif it will be quite satisfying, especially after the legs, eye, beak and wing edge have been embroidered.

Placing a central motif

Rule a frame around the outer edges of the motif and count the stitch width and depth. The bird illustrated

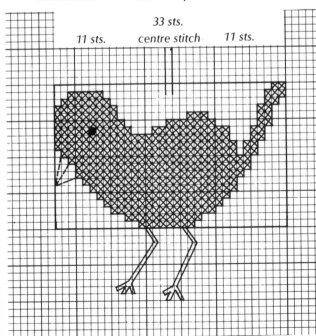

33 sts.

11 sts.   centre stitch   11 sts.

is 33 stitches wide and 20 rows deep (without legs). To find the centre stitch, divide 33 by 2. The 17th stitch counted from either edge of the motif is therefore the centre stitch. Mark this on the graph in a contrast colour and mark each motif square with a diagonal line. (These can be crossed off later as they are knitted.) On a graph page, mark out the total number of stitches required for the garment, find the centre stitch and place the 17th motif stitch directly above it.

The following example shows the bird motif worked on a garment 55 stitches wide. To find the centre stitch of the garment, divide 55 by 2. This gives 27 plus 1, indicating that the 28th stitch from either side is the centre stitch. The motif will therefore occupy 16 stitches on either side of the centre, leaving 11 stitches free.

If a written pattern is preferred, this can be calculated from the chart. Allow 8 rows for the legs to be embroidered, plus another 4 rows of stocking stitch above the top of the band. The motif should therefore commence on the 13th (or 15th) row above the band. Using the 55 stitches as a guide, read the chart from right to left for all knit rows and from left to right for all purl rows. It can be seen that 11 side stitches are required plus 13 stitches inside the frame on the first row. In this case, the motif is worked in blue on a white background.

1st row: K.24 wh., 12 bl., 22 wh.
2nd row: P.21 wh., 12 bl., 22 wh.
3rd row: K.21 wh., 15 bl., 19 wh.
4th row: P.18 wh., 17 bl., 20 wh.
5th row: K.19 wh., 19 bl., 17 wh.
6th row: P.16 wh., 21 bl., 18 wh.
7th row: K.18 wh., 22 bl., 15 wh.
8th row: P.14 wh., 24 bl., 17 wh.
9th row: K.16 wh., 25 bl., 14 wh.
10th row: P.13 wh., 26 bl., 16 wh.
11th row: K.15 wh., 2 bl., 1 wh., 25 bl., 12 wh.
12th row: P.11 wh., 26 bl., 1 wh., 2 bl., 15 wh.
13th row: K.14 wh., 2 bl., 3 wh., 25 bl., 11 wh.
14th row: P.11 wh., 11 bl., 3 wh., 11 bl., 3 wh., 2 bl., 14 wh.
15th row: K.13 wh., 2 bl., 6 wh., 7 bl., 6 wh., 10 bl., 11 wh.
16th row: P.11 wh., 9 bl., 10 wh., 3 bl., 7 wh., 2 bl., 13 wh.
17th row: K.13 wh., 2 bl., 20 wh., 9 bl., 11 wh.
18th row: P.12 wh., 7 bl., 2 wh., 2 bl., 12 wh.
19th row: K.11 wh., 3 bl., 23 wh., 5 bl., 13 wh.
20th row: P.31 wh., 2 bl., 11 wh.
Break off blue. Cont. in white only.

Placing two side-centre motifs

The following example uses 75 stitches overall with two bird motifs facing one another.

Graph out the bird again, in reverse. There are now two panels (motifs) of 33 stitches each to be placed equidistant over the garment. Using the previous method, the 38th stitch counted from either end is calculated as the centre stitch. Mark this on the graph of 75 stitches. There are now 37 side stitches and the motif occupies 33 stitches, with 4 remaining. Two of these are used for each side of the motif frame.

The complete graph now appears as follows (left to right): 2 stitches for the frame, 33 stitches for the first motif, 2 frame stitches, centre stitch, 2 frame stitches, 33 stitches for the second motif plus 2 frame stitches, making a total of 75.

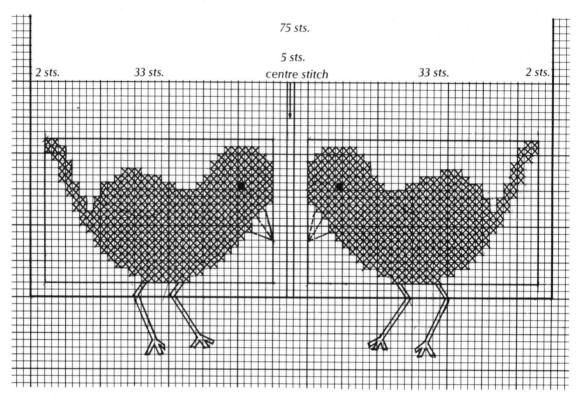

Where a band of Fair Isle is required in a repeated separate motif or a continuous design, see that the spacing enables the design to carry across the side seams in an uninterrupted pattern.

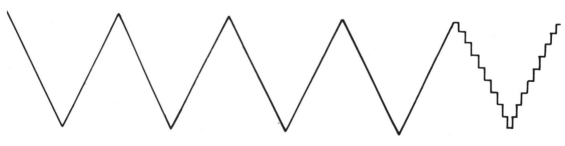

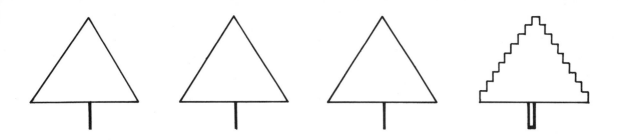

Example: The tree motif has 5 stitches between the widest points of each tree. Four stitches in the main colour would therefore be required at each end of the front and back to give a 5-stitch spacing across the side seams. This allows 2 stitches on each side to be absorbed into the seam. To work such a design in a 56 cm (22 in.) jumper where 63 stitches are required on both the front and back, the spacing for the design would be as follows:

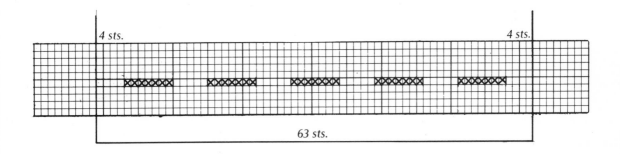

It will be necessary to experiment when draughting out the chosen design until it fits the required number of stitches. Use the number of stitches at the widest point and the number of stitches between each motif or design as the initial "key". If necessary, close or extend the gap by one or two stitches between designs and, when the spacing is stitch perfect, draw out the graph in its finished state.

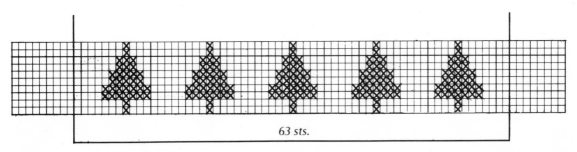

21

The following Fair Isle motifs are easy to work. The whiskers and fluffy tail of the rabbit are embroidered in after completion of the garment pieces. This pattern is easily transformed into a cat by shortening the ears and adding a tail. The cat motif requires only embroidered whiskers.

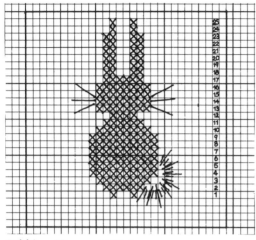

Rabbit — 25 rows × 10 sts.

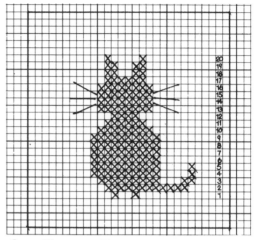

Cat — 20 rows × 15 sts.

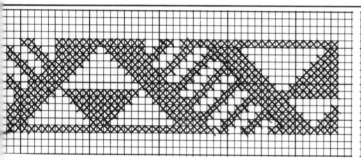

Some Maori designs from New Zealand

"Aramoana"

"Tukemata"

Aran knits

Aran knits are popular with all age groups and are equally suitable for males and females. The chunky cables and panels suggest the rugged outdoors, making them ideal for all winter sports.

The original Aran jerseys were made from natural or undyed, handspun wool and still are in many parts of the world. If this wool is available in your area, or if you can spin your own, you are fortunate indeed. However, many alternative wools are available to the handknitter which closely resemble the handspun. Aran knits can be made in any colour but traditionally the natural homespun shades of off-white through to brown-fleece shades are preferred. Avoid a flecked wool if possible, as this detracts from the Aran patterns.

The first part of this section introduces a selection of the cables and twists most frequently used. The Aran sampler includes the majority of these stitches and makes an ideal familiarisation course for those new to Aran knitting.

One complete pattern of an Aran knit averages between 8 to 28 rows. On completion of the first pattern it is not unusual to feel that it will be impossible to memorise the pattern rows. But after the second pattern repeat it will become familiar and soon it will be possible to knit from memory.

Arans usually have a simple panel of 8-10 cm 3½-4 ins.) along each side of the front, back and sleeves, whilst the main, central body part and the sleeves are patterned with cables and twists. The sleeves usually repeat a segment of the main body pattern. If working a design which includes several cables, it is advisable to use the instructions for the next larger chest size, as cables tend to hold in the work thus reducing the width.

For those not familiar with this type of knitting, a cable needle (size 4 mm) is required. A cable is produced by slipping a number of stitches from the left-hand needle on to the cable needle and holding these to the front or the back of the work. After working the required number of stitches from the left-hand needle, the stitches from the cable needle are worked. (It is advisable to stab the left-hand tip of the cable needle into the work to hold it firm when cabling to the front. With a back cable the cable needle will sit steady on its own.) Never twist or turn the stitches on a cable needle. Each time you cable back (cable needle held at the back of the work) the cable turns to the right. When you cable front (cable needle held at the front of the work) the cable turns to the left. Always read the detailed instructions of cables and twists given for an Aran pattern before commencing the pattern.

After completion of the sampler and with some help from the section on graphing a pattern, it will be possible to create original Aran designs.

Aran sampler

Materials: Two 50-gram balls of double-knitting wool. A pair of size 4 mm needles.
Cast on 40 sts. and work 8 rows moss st. thus:
1st row: (K.1, p.1) to end.
2nd row: Sl.1, (k.1, p.1) to end.
Keeping a 6-st. moss border up each side of the work, proceed as follows:

Single diamond

Section 1:
Abbreviations:
Tw.2 (Twist-2): K. into front of 2nd st. along l.h. needle then into front of 1st st., slipping both off l.h. needle together.
C.1f. (Cable 1 front): Sl. next st. onto cable needle, hold at front of work, p.1, then k. st. from cable needle.
C.1b. (Cable 1 back): Sl. next st. onto cable needle, hold at back of work, k.1, then p. st. from cable needle.
Note: When purling through the backs of the loops, or (as in twist front) knitting into the front of the second stitch first, use the tip of the right-hand needle to prise the stitch away from the left-hand needle, enabling the stitch to be worked with ease.
1st row: Moss 6, p.3, tw.2, p.3, k.1, p.10, k.1, p.3, tw.2, p.3, moss 6.
2nd row: Moss 6, k.3, p.2, k.3, p.1, k.10, p.1, k.3, p.2, k.3, moss 6.
3rd row: Moss 6, p.3, tw.2, p.3, c.1f., p.8, c.1b., p.3, tw.2, p.3, moss 6.
4th row: Moss 6, k.3, p.2, k.4, p.1, k.8, p.1, k.4, p.2, k.3, moss 6.
5th row: Moss 6, p.3, tw.2, p.4, c.1f., p.6, c.1b., p.4, tw.2, p.3, moss 6.
6th row: Moss 6, k.3, p.2, k.5, p.1, k.6, p.1, k.5, p.2, k.3, moss 6.
7th row: Moss 6, p.3, tw.2, p.5, c.1f., p.4, c.1b., p.5, tw.2, p.3, moss 6.
8th row: Moss 6, k.3, p.2, k.6, p.1, k.4, p.1, k.6, p.2, k.3, moss 6.
9th row: Moss 6, p.3, tw.2, p.6, c.1f., p.2, c.1b., p.6, tw.2, p.3, moss 6.
10th row: Moss 6, k.3, p.2, k.7, p.1, k.2, p.1, k.7, p.2, k.3, moss 6.
11th row: Moss 6, p.3, tw.2, p.7, c.1f., c.1b., p.7, tw.2, p.3, moss 6.
12th row: Moss 6, k.3, p.2, k.8, p.2, k.8, p.2, k.3, moss 6.

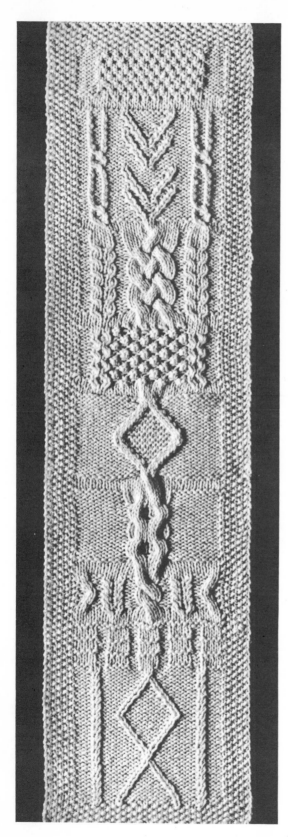

13th row: Moss 6, p.3, tw.2, p.8, tw.2, p.8, tw.2, p.3, moss 6.

14th row: Moss 6, k.3, p.2, k.8, p.2, k.8, p.2, k.3, moss 6.

15th row: Moss 6, p.3, tw.2, p.7, c.1b., c.1f., p.7, tw.2, p.3, moss 6.

16th row: Moss 6, k.3, p.2, k.7, p.1, k.2, p.1, k.7, p.2, k.3, moss 6.

17th row: Moss 6, p.3, tw.2, p.6, c.1b., p.2, c.1f., p.6, tw.2, p.3, moss 6.

18th row: Moss 6, k.3, p.2, k.6, p.1, k.4, p.1, k.6, p.2, k.3, moss 6.

19th row: Moss 6, p.3, tw.2, p.5, c.1b., p.4, c.1f., p.5, tw.2, p.3, moss 6.

20th row: Moss 6, k.3, p.2, k.5, p.1, k.6, p.1, k.5, p.2, k.3, moss 6.

21st row: Moss 6, p.3, tw.2, p.4, c.1b., p.6, c.1f., p.4, tw.2, p.3, moss 6.

22nd row: Moss 6, k.3, p.2, k.4, p.1, k.8, p.1, k.4, p.2, k.3, moss 6.

23rd row: Moss 6, p.3, tw.2, p.3, c.1b., p.8, c.1f., p.3, tw.2, p.3, moss 6.

24th row: Moss 6, k.3, p.2, k.3, p.1, k.10, p.1, k.3, p.2, k.3, moss 6.

25th row: Moss 6, p.3, tw.2, p.3, c.1f., p.8, c.1b., p.3, tw.2, p.3, moss 6.

26th row: Moss 6, k.3, p.2, k.4, p.1, k.8, p.1, k.4, p.2, k.3, moss 6.

27th row: Moss 6, p.3, tw.2, p.4, c.1f., p.6, c.1b., p.4, tw.2, p.3, moss 6.

28th row: Moss 6, k.3, p.2, k.5, p.1, k.6, p.1, k.5, p.2, k.3, moss 6.

29th row: Moss 6, p.3, tw.2, p.5, c.1f., p.4, c.1b., p.5, tw.2, p.3, moss 6.

30th row: Moss 6, k.3, p.3, k.6, p.1, k.4, p.1, k.6, p.2, k.3, moss 6.

31st row: Moss 6, p.3, tw.2, p.6, c.1f., p.2, c.1b., p.6, tw.2, p.3, moss 6.

32nd row: Moss 6, k.3, p.2, k.7, p.1, k.2, p.1, k.7, p.2, k.3, moss 6.

33rd row: Moss 6, p.3, tw.2, p.7, c.1f., c.1b., p.7, tw.2, p.3, moss 6.

34th row: Moss 6, k.3, p.2, k.8, p.2, k.8, p.2, k.3, moss 6.

35th row: Moss 6, p.3, tw.2, p.8, tw.2, p.8, tw.2, p.3, moss 6.

36th row: Moss 6, k.3, p.2, k.8, p.2, k.8, p.3, k.3, moss 6.

If this pattern is to be continued, repeat rows 15-36 for the length required. This would make an attractive scarf, finishing with the diamond open (V) to match up with the opposite end.

Plate 10

Plate 14

Plate 15

Section 2: broken rib

This is one of the most frequently-used side-panel stiches and is also popular as a smaller patterned strip in Aran knitting. Retain the 6-st. moss border.
1st row: Moss 6, (k.4, p.2) 4 times, k.4, moss 6.
2nd row: Moss 6, (p.4, k.2) 4 times, k.4, moss 6.
3rd row: As 1st row.
4th row: Moss 6, k. to last 6 sts., moss 6.
Repeat 1st-4th rows twice.

There are many adaptations of this broken rib. It can also look most attractive with a twist-2 between each plain section in place of the knit 2 here.

Section 3: double twist-2, central 6-stitch cable, side half-cables

Work 4 rows stst. with the moss st. border to divide work before commencing this section.
Abbreviations:
C.2f. (Cable 2 front): Sl. next 2 sts. onto cable needle and hold at front of work. P. next 2 sts., then k.2 sts. from cable needle.
C.2b. (Cable 2 back): Sl. next st. onto cable needle and hold at back of work. K. next 2 sts. then p. st. from cable needle.
Tw.2b. (Twist-2 back): K. into back (t.b.l.) of 2nd st. along l.h. needle, then k. into front of 1st st. slipping both off l.h. needle together.
Tw.2f. (Twist-2 front): Exactly as per tw.2 in first pattern of sampler.
C.3f. (Cable 3 front): Sl. next 3 sts. onto cable needle. Hold at front of work. K. next 3 sts. then k.3 sts. from cable needle.

1st row: Moss 6, k.2, p.3, tw.2f., tw.2b., p.2, k.6, p.2, tw.2f., tw.2b., p.3, k.2, moss 6.
2nd row: Moss 6, p.2, k.3, p.4, k.2, p.6, k.2, p.4, k.3, p.2, moss 6.
3rd row: Moss 6, c.2f., p.2, tw.2f., tw.2b., p.2, c.3f., p.2, tw.2f., tw.2b., p.2, c.2b, moss 6.
4th row: Moss 6, k.2, p.1, k.2, p.4, k.2, p.6, k.2, p.4, k.2, p.2, k.1, moss 6.
5th row: Moss 6, p.1, c.2f., p.1, tw.2f., tw.2b., p.2, k.6, p.2, tw.2f., tw.2b., p.1, c.2b., p.1, moss 6.
6th row: Moss 6, k.2, p.2, k.1, p.4, k.2, p.6, k.2, p.4, k.1, p.2, k.2, moss 6.
7th row: Moss 6, p.1, c.2b., p.1, tw.2f., tw.2b., p.2, k.6, p.2, tw.2f., tw.2b., p.1, c.2f., p.1, moss 6.
8th row: Moss 6, k.1, p.2, k.2, p.4, k.2, p.6, k.2, p.4, k.2, p.2, k.1, moss 6.
9th row: Moss 6, c.2b., p.2, tw.2f., tw.2b., p.2, c.3f., p.2, tw.2f., tw.2b., p.2, c.2f., moss 6.
10th row: Moss 6, p.2, k.3, p.4, k.2, p.6, k.2, p.4, k.3, p.2, moss 6.

Work 4 rows stst. (with moss st. borders) to divide work.

Section 4: two-layered cable

This cable is far too attractive to be submerged into the depths of other stitches and it is therefore bordered here with a broad band of reversed stocking stitch, to bring it into maximum relief. It is a recommended cable to use as a central panel (approximately 18 stitches wide) with reversed stocking stitch on either side and the remainder of the jumper in plain stocking stitch, or as two side panels between plain stocking stitch.

Abbreviations:
C.6b. (Cable 6 back): Sl. next 3 sts. onto cable needle. Hold at back of work. K. next 3 sts., then k.3 sts. from cable needle.
C.6f. (Cable 6 front): Sl. next 3 sts. onto cable needle. Hold at front of work. K. next 3 sts., then k.3 sts. from cable needle.

1st row: Moss 6, p.8, k.12, p.8, moss 6.
2nd row: Moss 6, k.8, p.12, k.8, moss 6.
These 2 rows "set" the pattern.
3rd row: Moss 6, p.8, c.6b., c.6f., p.8, moss 6.
4th row: Moss 6, k.8, p.12, k.8, moss 6.
5th row: Moss 6, p.8, k.12, p.8, moss 6.
6th row: Moss 6, k.8, p.12, k.8, moss 6.
7th row: Moss 6, p.8, c.6f., c.6b., p.8, moss 6.
8th row: Moss 6, k.8, p.12, k.8, moss 6.
9th row: Moss 6, p.8, k.12, p.8, moss 6.
10th row: Moss 6, k.8, p.12, k.8, moss 6.
11th row: Moss 6, p.8, k.12, p.8, moss 6.
12th row: Moss 6, k.8, p.12, k.8, moss 6.
Repeat the 3rd-10th rows (incl.) once more.
Work 4 rows stst. with moss st. borders.

Section 5: twisted diamond with garter stitch insert

Abbreviations:
C.4f. (Cable 4 front): Sl. next 2 sts. onto cable needle and hold at front of work. K. next 2 sts. t.b.l., then k.2 sts. from cable needle t.b.l.
C.3b. (Cable 3 back): Sl. next st. onto cable needle and hold at back of work. K. next 2 sts. t.b.l., then k. st. from cable needle.
C.3f. (Cable 3 front): Sl. next 2 sts. onto cable needle and hold at front of work. K. next st., then k.2 sts. t.b.l. from cable needle.

1st row: Moss 6, p.12, c.4f., p.12, moss 6.
2nd row: Moss 6, k.12, p.4 t.b.l., k.12, moss 6.
3rd row: Moss 6, p.11, c.3b., c.3f., p.11, moss 6.
4th row: Moss 6, k.11, p.2 t.b.l., k.2, p.2 t.b.l., k.11, moss 6.
5th row: Moss 6, p.10, c.3b., k.2, c.3f., p.10, moss 6.
6th row: Moss 6, k.10, p.2 t.b.l., k.4, p.2 t.b.l., k.10, moss 6.
7th row: Moss 6, p.9, c.3b., k.4, c.3f., p.9, moss 6.

8th row: Moss 6, k.9, p.2 t.b.l., k.6, p.2 t.b.l., k.9, moss 6.
9th row: Moss 6, p.8, c.3b., k.6, c.3f., p.8, moss 6.
10th row: Moss 6, k.8, p.2 t.b.l., k.8, p.2 t.b.l., k.8, moss 6.
11th row: Moss 6, p.7, c.3b., k.8, c.3f., p.7, moss 6.
12th row: Moss 6, k.7, p.2 t.b.l., k.10, p.2 t.b.l., k.7, moss 6.
13th row: Moss 6, p.7, k.2 t.b.l., k.10, k.2 t.b.l., p.7, moss 6.
14th row: As 12th row.
15th row: Moss 6, p.7, c.3f., k.8, c.3b., p.7, moss 6.
16th row: As 10th row.
17th row: Moss 6, p.8, c.3f., k.6, c.3b., p.8, moss 6.
18th row: As 8th row.
19th row: Moss 6, p.9, c.3f., k.4, c.3b., p.9, moss 6.
20th row: As 6th row.
21st row: Moss 6, p.10, c.3f., k.2, c.3b., p.10, moss 6.
22nd row: As 4th row.
23rd row: Moss 6, p.11, c.3f., c.3b., p.11, moss 6.
24th row: As 2nd row.

These instructions give one complete pattern. If this is used as an overall pattern, repeat these 24 rows for the length required.

Work 4 rows stst. with moss st. border.

Section 6: bramble stitch centre panel and mock cable

Abbreviations:
Tw.2f. (Twist-2 front): K. into front of 2nd st., then k. into front of 1st st., slipping both sts. off needle together.
Tw.2b. (Twist-2 back): K. into back of 2nd st., then k. into front of 1st st., slipping both sts. off needle together.

1st row: Moss 6, p.2, tw.2f., tw.2b., p.16, tw.2f., tw.2b., p.2, moss 6.
2nd row: Moss 6, k.2, p.4, (k.1, p.1, k.1 all into next st., p. next 3 sts. tog.) 4 times, p.4, k.2, moss 6.
3rd row: Moss 6, p.2, tw.2b., tw.2f., p.16, tw.2b., tw.2f., p.2, moss 6.
4th row: Moss 6, k.2, p.4, (p.3 tog., k.1, p.1, k.1 into next st.) 4 times, p.4, k.2, moss 6.

Repeat these 4 rows three times.
Work 4 rows stst. with moss st. borders.

The knobbly centre panel has many names, two of the most popular being "bramble stitch" and "berry stitch". Alternating the twist-2 front and twist-2 back sections turns this versatile stitch into a mock cable. This could be easily improved by inserting reversed stocking stitch on either side of the cable, but for this sampler it serves as an illustration and for practice. In the next section there is an even further version of the twist-2 stitch.

Section 7: chunky cable

Abbreviations:
Tw.2f. (Twist-2 front): As per instructions in the previous section.
Tw.2b. (Twist-2 back): As per instructions in the previous section.
C.3f. (Cable 3 front): Sl. next 3 sts. onto cable needle. Hold in front of work. K. next 3 sts., then k.3 sts. from cable needle.
C.3b. (Cable 3 back): Sl. next 3 sts. onto cable needle. Hold at back of work. K. next 3 sts., then k.3 sts. from cable needle.

1st row: Moss 6, p.2, tw.2f., tw.2b., p.2, k.12, p.2, tw.2f., tw.2b., p.2, moss 6.
2nd row: Moss 6, k.2, p.4, k.2, p.12, k.2, p.4, k.2, moss 6.
3rd row: Moss 6, p.2, k.4, p.2, (c.3f.) twice, p.2, k.4, p.2, moss 6.
4th row: Moss 6, k.2, p.4, k.2, p.12, k.2, p.4, k.2, moss 6.
5th row: As 1st row.
6th row: As 2nd row.
7th row: Moss 6, p.2, k.4, p.2, k.3, c.3b., k.3, p.2, k.4, p.2, moss 6.
8th row: Moss 6, k.2, p.4, k.2, p.12, k.2, p.4, k.2, moss 6.

Repeat these 8 rows twice.
Work 4 rows stst. with moss st. borders.

Section 8: single v-cable and single side-cables

Abbreviations:
C.4f. (Cable 4 front): Sl. next st. onto cable needle. Hold in front of work. K.1 t.b.l., p.2, then k. t.b.l. the st. from cable needle.

1st row: Moss 6, p.2, c.4f., p.7, k.2, p.7, c.4f., p.2, moss 6.
2nd row: Moss 6, k.2, p.4, k.7, p.2, k.7, p.4, k.2, moss 6.
3rd row: Moss 6, p.2, (k.1 t.b.l., p.2) twice, p.4, tw.2f., tw.2b., p.6, (k.1 t.b.l., p.2) twice, moss 6.
4th row: Moss 6, k.2, (p.1 t.b.l., k.2) twice, k.4, p.1, k.2, p.1, k.6, (p.1 t.b.l., k.2) twice, moss 6.
5th row: Moss 6, p.2, c.4f., p.5, tw.2f., p.2, tw.2b., p.5, c.4f., p.2, moss 6.
6th row: Moss 6, k.2, (p.1 t.b.l., k.2) twice, k.3, p.1, k.4, p.1, k.5, (p.1 t.b.l., k.2) twice, moss 6.
7th row: Moss 6, p.2, (k.1 t.b.l., p.2) twice, p.2, tw.2f., p.1, k.2, p.1, tw.2b., p.4, (k.1 t.b.l., p.2) twice, moss 6.
8th row: Moss 6, k.2, (p.1 t.b.l., k.2) twice, k.2, p.1, k.2, p.2, k.2, p.1, k.4, (p.1 t.b.l., k.2) twice, moss 6.
9th row: Moss 6, p.2, (k.1 t.b.l., p.2) twice, p.1, tw.2f., p.1, tw.2f., tw.2b., p.1, tw.2b., p.3, (k.1 t.b.l., p.2) twice, moss 6.

10th row: Moss 6, k.2, (p.1 t.b.l., k.2) twice, k.1, p.1, (k.2, p.1) twice, k.1, p.1, k.4, (p.1 t.b.l., k.2) twice, moss 6.

11th row: Moss 6, p.2, (k.1 t.b.l., p.2) twice, p.3, tw.2f., p.2, tw.2b., p.5, (k.1 t.b.l., p.2) twice, moss 6.

12th row: Moss 6, k.2, (p.1 t.b.l., k.2) twice, k.3, p.1, k.4, p.1, k.5, (p.1 t.b.l., k.2) twice, moss 6.

13th row: Moss 6, p.2, (k.1 t.b.l., p.2) twice, p.2, tw.2f., p.4, tw.2b., p.4, (k.1 t.b.l., p.2) twice, moss 6.

14th row: Moss 6, k.2, (p.1 t.b.l., k.2) twice, k.2, p.1, k.6, p.1, k.4, (p.1 t.b.l., k.2) twice, moss 6.

15th row: Moss 6, p.2, (k.1 t.b.l., p.2) twice, p.1, tw.2f., p.6, tw.2b., p.3, (k.2 t.b.l., p.2) twice, moss 6.

16th row: Moss 6, k.2, (p.1 t.b.l., k.2) twice, k.1, p.1, k.8, p.1, k.3, (p.1 t.b.l., k.2) twice, moss 6.

Repeat these 16 rows once.

It can now be seen that the central single-cable double-v effect has been completed, not by the same method as was used in the first section, but by the now-familiar twist-2 front and twist-2 back method.

Section 9: double moss

This is a frequently-used side-panel stitch in Aran knits. Double moss is simply two rows of the first moss stitch row before changing over. This can be seen clearly as the work progresses. Retain (single) moss stitch borders.

1st row: Moss 6, p.4, (k.1, p.1) 10 times, p.4, moss 6.
2nd row: Moss 6, k.4, (k.1, p.1) 10 times, k.4, moss 6.
3rd row: Moss 6, p.4, (p.1, k.1) 10 times, p.4, moss 6.
4th row: Moss 6, k.4, (p.1, k.1) 10 times, k.4, moss 6.

Repeat these 4 rows twice, then repeat rows 1 and 2.

Now work 8 rows of single moss to match the lower edge of the sampler and cast off.

It is suggested that this sampler is kept intact for consultation regarding the various twists or cables when graphing out patterns. Many of these stitches are delightful on their own, the double moss being particularly attractive for babies' and young children's knitwear.

4. The basic knitting companion

How to use the basic patterns

This section demonstrates how to follow the basic patterns and how these can be varied to make virtually any garment. It also includes written instructions for some of the author's variations which can be used as they appear, or can be adapted to suit the required chest size.

The first decision concerns whether double-knitting or 4-ply wool is to be used. Double-knitting wool is warmer, quicker to knit, perhaps longer wearing and more functional for everyday wear or for colder climates. Four-ply, being finer and requiring smaller needles, will take longer to knit but is certainly the winner for a fashion garment. Machine knitters will find the 4-ply section ideal, although those without ribbing attachments should deduct the front border stitches from the basic patterns and work the borders separately.

Secondly, check the chest size and underarm measurements of the recipient and decide between raglan and set-in sleeves. If a short-sleeved garment is to be worked and the recipient has thin upper arms, cast on 4 stitches less than the stated number for double-knit and 6 stitches less for 4-ply. Work the cuff as per the basic instructions but increase the amount of stitches evenly by the number deducted across the last cuff row.

Next turn to the appropriate "wool required" guide (pages 51 to 52). Also check the correct needle size.

The basic patterns in chest sizes 46 to 117 cm (18 to 46 in.) are in the back of this book in two distinct parts, double-knit and 4-ply. Each part has been divided into five sections for easy reference (back patterns, fronts, sleeves, collars and neckbands, and tank-tops).

Turn to the double-knit or 4-ply section and check the appropriate chest size. Do not hesitate to add or reduce one stitch to fit the stitch-pattern layout.

1. Knit a tension swatch in stocking stitch on the larger-sized needles to be used. Refer to the tension diagram in the first part of this book. If the tension is incorrect adjust the needle size to suit.
2. If working Fair Isle, a patterned panel or an Aran knit, chart the design on graph paper as outlined in Chapter 3.
3. Commence with the back. These instructions are for any type of garment but the length must be modified if working a jacket, jerkin or tunic (see pages 30 and 46). Work to the armhole, then follow either the raglan or set-in sleeve instructions.
4. Knit the front(s) of the style you have chosen. Pay particular attention to the information on page 6 if knitting a high or v-necked cardigan.
5. Knit the sleeves from either the long-sleeve or short-sleeve instructions with raglan or set-in armholes, as chosen.
6. Work the neckband or collar of your choice. Note: If a collar is preferred to the round neck given for all the high-necked cardigans, simply disregard the round-neck instructions and substitute the collar pattern from the lumberjacket instructions.

See notes on pressing, finishing etc. (page 4) before sewing up.

Double-knitting

Belted jackets and jerkins (in double-knit)

Both the v-neck and the basic cardigan patterns can be easily adapted to make sleeveless or long-sleeved jackets or jerkins.

If a pattern is being extended to make a jacket or jerkin with long sleeves, allow one extra 50-gram ball of wool for sizes 61-66 cm (24-26 in.), two 50-gram balls for sizes 71-86 cm (27-34 in.) and three 50-gram balls for sizes 91-117 cm (36-46 in.).

If knitting a sleeveless version of any basic pattern, deduct one 50-gram ball from the quantities given for a long-sleeved garment for small sizes, two 50-gram balls for medium sizes and three 50-gram balls for large sizes. Use the armband pattern given for the sleeveless v-necked jumper. These calculations should include sufficient wool for a plain belt and crocheted or plaited belt loops. (Instructions below.)

To lengthen the basic pattern: Commence at the lower edge of the back and front(s). Using 4 mm needles, cast on the required number of stitches. Work 4 rows rib or a full ribbed band if preferred. Change to 4½ mm needles and commence the main pattern, working an extra 6.5-6.7 cm (2½-3 in.) for all sizes up to 71 cm (28 in.) chest. For sizes 76-117 cm (30-46 in.) add an extra 10-12.75 cm (4-5 in.). Change back to 4 mm needles and continue in pattern to the armhole, adding the extra length to the instructions.

Belt: Using 3½ mm needles cast on 8 sts. and rib to match the bands for the length required.

Belt with buckle or dome fasteners: Work for waist measurement plus 10 cm (4 in.).

Tie-belt: (Allow one extra 50-gram ball for a tie-belt.) Work for waist measurement plus 102 cm (40 in.) for small and medium sizes, or 122 cm (48 in.) for larger sizes.

Belt loops: Crochet, plait or knit these and fix them firmly at the waistline of the garment.

Knitted belt loops: Using 3½ mm needles, cast on 3 sts. and rib as follows:

1st row: Sl.1, k.1, p.1.
2nd row: Sl.1, p.1, k.1 for 4 cm (1½ in.).

Knitted belt loops can be made a feature of the garment if a set of six are made and placed at the side seams, centre-side fronts and centre-side backs.

A word on lumberjackets

The double-opening (or double-ended) zip fasteners which are required for lumberjackets are not always available in the length and colour required. If the only suitable fastener is a little short, use the following method to overcome the problem. The zip should be placed so that the lumberjacket fronts can be closed right up to the neck, even though this garment is usually worn slightly unzipped. If the zip is a little short, the gap at the lower edges can be hidden by knitting a tab with a buttonhole in one side. Stitch the tab to one front band with a button and sew a matching button to the other side so that the tab may be buttoned across.

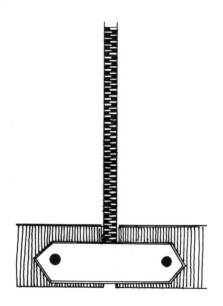

If the zip is exceptionally short, an additional tab can be placed across the neck just under the collar.

Tab (all sizes): (Read across chart from left to right)

	4-ply	Double knit	
On size	2¾ mm	3¼ mm needles	
Cast on 1 st. Working in k.1, p.1 rib, inc. each end of every alt. row until there are	15	11	sts.
Cont. straight until tab measures	7.75	7.75	cm
	3	3	in.
Buttonhole: Rib	6	4	sts.
Cast off next 3 sts., rib to end.			
Next row: Rib	6	4	sts.
Cast on 3 sts., rib to end.			
Dec. 1 st. at each end of every alt. row until 1 st. remains. Fasten off.			

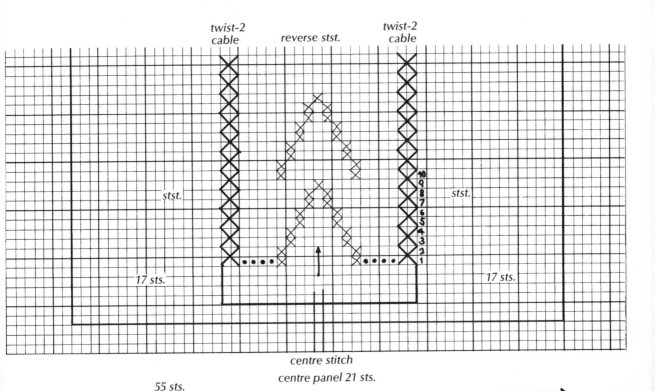

twist-2 cable   reverse stst.   twist-2 cable

stst.   stst.

17 sts.   17 sts.

centre stitch

centre panel 21 sts.

55 sts.

Variations on the double-knit patterns

This is a selection of the author's variations on the basic patterns at the back of the book, demonstrating only a few of the many ways in which individual touches can make a garment truly unique.

"Aaron" (see plate 1)

A mini Aran knit made for a size 46cm (18in.) chest from the basic raglan-sleeved, crew-necked pattern.

The working graph shows how the centre panel was devised.

The pattern reads as follows:
Abbreviations:
C.f. (Cable front): Sl. next st. onto cable needle. Place in front of work, p. next st., then k. st. from cable needle.
C.b. (Cable back): As above, placing the st. on the cable needle at back of work.
Tw.2 (Twist-2): K. into the back of the 2nd st. along l.h. needle, then k. into the front of the 1st st., slipping both loops off needle together.
After completion of the band:
1st row: K.16, tw.2, p.4, k.1, p.7, k.1, p.4, tw.2, k.16.
2nd row: P.18, k.4, p.1, k.7, p.1, k.4, p.18.
3rd row: K.16, tw.2, p.4, c.f., p.5, c.b., p.4, tw.2, k.16.
4th row: P.18, k.5, p.1, k.5, p.1, k.5, p.18.
5th row: K.16, tw.2, p.5, c.f., p.3, c.b., p.5, tw.2, k.16.

6th row: P.18, k.6, p.1, k.3, p.1, k.6, p.18.
7th row: K.16, tw.2, p.6, c.f., p.1, c.b., p.6, tw.2, k.16.
8th row: P.18, k.7, p.1, k.1, p.1, k.7, p.18.
9th row: K.16, tw.2, p.7, make 1 (by purling into loop between sts. of previous row), k.3 tog., make 1, p.7, tw.2, k.16.
10th row: P.18, k.8, p.1, k.8, p.18.

These 10 rows form one pattern. Repeat them for the desired length.

The Aran panel is begun on the first row worked on 4 mm needles, and is carried up to the neck. Follow the shaping instructions specified at the back of the book for the back, front, sleeves and neckband, keeping the Aran work "set" correctly. (It will be necessary to adjust the number of stitches on either side of the Aran panel as the armhole shapings are made.)

If you wish to work this panel on a v-necked or polo-necked garment, or a cardigan, simply follow the appropriate shaping instructions at the back of the book. Similarly, the panel can be worked on a larger-sized garment by increasing the number of knit and purl stitches at each side until you have the specified number. If the garment is several times larger, it might be more appropriate to repeat the panel. A new pattern should then be graphed to ensure the panels are equidistant from the centre and edges.

31

"Coral" (see plate 2)

A cardigan knitted in the 46cm (18in.) chest size specifying 55 stitches. (Because an even number of stitches were required for the lace pattern, the stitch numbers for the fronts and back were reduced by one.)

The pattern for the attractive lacy bands around the base of the cardigan and sleeves reads as follows:
K.4 rows stst.
5th row: K.1, (wl.fwd., k.2 tog.) to last st., k.1.
6th row: P.
7th row: K.2, (wl.fwd., k.2 tog.) to end.
8th row: P.

These 8 rows complete one pattern. They should be begun directly after the bands have been worked on the back, fronts and sleeves, and repeated for the length required.

This pattern could be applied equally well to larger sizes with an even stitch count, or it could be used effectively over the entire body of the garment.

"Coconut ice" (see plate 3)

A cosy little jersey worked from the basic raglan-sleeved, high-necked cardigan pattern in size 46 cm (18in.). The illustrated example was worked in pink and cream, but it would be equally attractive in a single colour.

Because the chosen stitch pattern requires an even number of stitches and the pattern quotes an uneven number, the following compromise should be made: an extra stitch should be added to the back and 1 stitch should be deducted from each of the fronts. The 2 x 2 ribbing complements the stitch pattern nicely.

Follow the basic instructions given at the back of the book remembering to add or subtract 1 stitch from the back and front as appropriate. Insert the following after completion of the back and front bands: (r.s.f.)

Back and left front
*P. 4 rows (white).
P. 1 row (pink).
Work 2 x 2 rib for 3 rows in pink. Rept. from * to end.
(This gives a clear, raised contrast for the garter stitch stripes which are worked right through the raglan shapings in purl.)

The pattern must be reversed for the right front giving the following instructions:
*K. 4 rows (white)
K. 1 row (pink).
Work 2 x 2 rib for 3 rows in pink. Rept. from * to end.

Sleeves
Work as per basic instructions in plain stocking stitch in pink.

The buttonholes coincide with the centre rows of each white stripe, making buttonhole spacing on the front borders easy. The number of buttons may be reduced if desired, however (see buttonhole section on page 6).

"Amanda" (see plate 4)

A short-sleeved raglan jumper knitted in size 71cm (28in.). This garment features bands and a collar in moss stitch. The main body is worked in reversed stocking stitch featuring a panel 19 stitches wide on the centre front and sleeves, with reversed stocking stitch diamonds. There are 8 rows of stocking stitch between the diamonds.

The patterned panel reads as follows:
1st row: K.9, p.1, k.9.
2nd row: P.8, k.3, p.8.

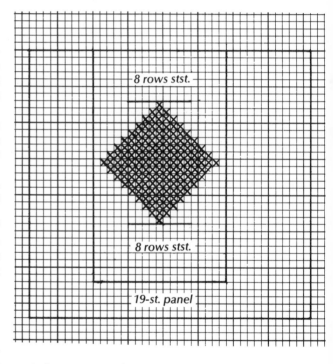

8 rows stst.

8 rows stst.

19-st. panel

3rd row: K.7, p.5, k.7.
4th row: P.6, k.7, p.6.
5th row: K.5, p.9, k.5.
6th row: P.4, k.11, p.4.
7th row: K.3, p.13, k.3.
8th row: P.2, k.15, p.2.
9th row: K.1, p.17, k.1.
10th row: As 8th row.
11th row: As 7th row.
12th row: As 6th row.
13th row: As 5th row.

14th row: As 4th row.
15th row: As 3rd row.
16th row: As 2nd row.
17th row: As 1st row.
18th row: P.19.

Work a further 8 rows stst. in the panel before comencing the next diamond.

Before beginning work, calculate the centre of the pattern and ensure that it is placed equidistant from the edges of the garment piece (see page 9). This garment has 29 stitches on either side of the panel and the first pattern row (after working the band and 8 rows stst.) would therefore read: k.38, p.1, k.38. (Adjust the width of the stocking stitch side panels if you wish to work a larger garment.)

The placing of marker threads at the outer edges of the patterned panel would cancel the need to calculate complete instructions for individual rows. When the pattern becomes clearly visible these threads can be removed.

"Craig" (see plate 5)

Knitted in size 71 cm (28 in.) with raglan sleeves, this double-knit turtle-necked jersey has a plain back and sleeves. The front features alternating wide stripes and a checkerboard design in gold and white.

Follow the basic pattern instructions for the back, sleeves and neckband.

Front
On completion of the band work as follows:
1st row: (K.3 gold, 3 white) to end of row, finish with 3 gold.
2nd row: P. as 1st row.
3rd row: As 1st row.
4th row: As 2nd row.
5th row: (K.3 white, 3 gold) to end of row, finish with 3 white.
6th row: P. as 5th row.
7th row: As 5th row.
8th row: As 6th row.
9th-12th rows: As 1st-4th rows. Break off gold.
Work 12 rows stst. in white.
Work 12 rows stst. in gold.
Repeat from * once, noting that the armhole commences directly after the second 12 rows of white have been worked.

Repeat the checkerboard pattern and the 12 white rows once. Break off the white wool and complete the remainder of the front in gold.

For a larger size, follow the appropriate basic instructions, ensuring that the stitch number for the front is divisible by three to accommodate the checkerboard pattern. Add or subtract a stitch if necessary.

"Trudi" (see plate 5)

A tank top in size 81 cm (32 in.) featuring combined Fair Isle and embroidery. The graph shows the design for the flower-pot, but this may be embroidered or omitted altogether.

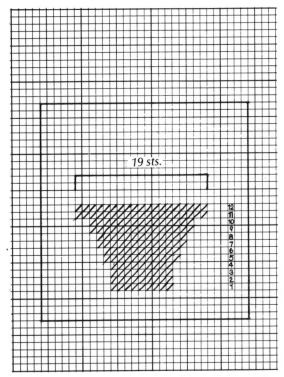

4 rows stst. above band

Work the back, neckband and armbands as specified in the basic pattern for the appropriate size. Centre the Fair Isle on the front as outlined in the section on graphing Fair Isle (page 18) and, after completing the band, work 4 rows in plain stocking stitch before beginning the pattern. (The illustrated example also shows two contrasting bands of colour in the ribbed section.)

When the front is completed work the embroidery. Trace the flowers (see over page) on to smooth tissue paper, align the drawing with the top of the flower-pot and tack it all around. Embroider over the tissue, tearing the paper away when completed.

"Colleen" (see plate 6)

A green skinny-rib jumper adapted from the 91 cm (36 in.) long-sleeved, polo-necked pattern. With the body of the garment worked mainly in k.2, p.2 rib, this jumper features bands of vertical white and green stripes at the waist, cuffs and polo neck.

Follow the basic pattern instructions for the back and front, disregarding the initial ribbed band. Begin with 4 mm needles and work 2 × 2 rib (k.2, p.2) in green wool until the work matches the hip to waist-line measurement. Change to 3¼ mm needles and work 12 rows stst. as follows:
1st row: K.2 white, (2 green, 2 white) to end.
2nd row: P.2 white, (2 green, 2 white) to end.
Rept. these 2 rows 5 times.
Change back to 4 mm needles and cont. in 2 × 2 rib as before.

Sleeves: Follow the basic instructions for the desired size, substituting the initial ribbed bands with the following: After casting on the required number of stitches in green wool, work 2 rows stst. Work the bands of vertical white and green stripes in stst. as follows:
Next row: K.2 white (2 green, 2 white) to end.
Next row: P.2 white (2 green, 2 white) to end.
Rept. these 2 rows 5 times.

Change to 4 mm needles and continue working the sleeve in 2 × 2 rib with green wool as before.

Polo neck: Follow the basic pattern instructions, substituting the ribbing with green and white vertical stripes in stst. as outlined above.

When the work is 1 cm (⅜ in.) shorter than the desired length, break off the white wool and work 2 rows of stst. in green. Cast off in green.

"Hans" (see plate 7)

This attractive ski sweater was knitted in navy and white in a 4 × 1 rib (k.4, p.1) up to the white striped section on the back, front and sleeves. The top raglan sections are knitted in stocking stitch.

Follow the appropriate back, front and sleeve instructions until the work measures 5 cm (2 in.) short of the bottom to underarm length. Work 2 rows stst. in navy wool, then work in stst. as follows:
2 rows white
2 rows navy
1 row white
3 rows navy
2 rows white
2 rows white/navy checkerboard (2 white, 2 navy).
Break off white.

Back and sleeves only:
Cont. in stst. in navy, working raglan sections as specified in the basic instructions.

Front:
Fair Isle motif: the snowflake motif is worked on the front of the garment only.

Placing: If a crew or turtle-necked jumper is being made, commence the motif 8 stst. rows above the white/navy checkerboard. If it is to be a polo-necked garment, commence the motif 16 stst. rows above the checkerboard. This will set the snowflake equidistant between the checkerboard and the top of the chosen neckline. A small amount of red wool is required.

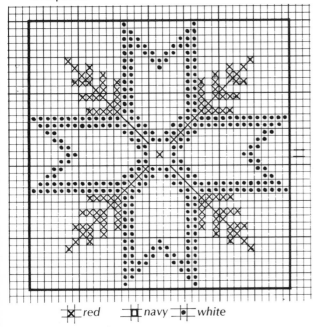

☒red ⊡navy ⊡white

The graph shows that the motif is worked over 37 stitches and 37 rows.

To avoid tangles, use two small balls of red wool on either side of the design. This colour is only required for the odd stitch, so attach the balls to the back of the work with a safety-pin, unwinding the wool as required.

Centre the motif with the help of the graph and mark the "frame" with two threads of contrast wool. (It is advisable to do this several rows before the motif begins, bringing the frame threads up each row and flipping them to the side between two stitches. This enables the exact number of main-colour stitches which have been worked inside the frame to be calculated.) Remove the frame threads when the motif is completed.

Work as follows (N.B. These instructions are for the stitches inside the frame only): Add the appropriate number of side stitches according to the garment size, and continue the raglan shapings throughout.

Abbreviations: N., navy; wh., white; r., red.

Bring the frame marker threads up through each row.

1st row: K.13 n., 1 wh., 9 n., 1 wh., 13 n.

2nd row: P.13 n., 2 wh., 7 n., 2 wh., 13 n.
3rd row: K.13 n., 3 wh., 5 n., 3 wh., 13 n.
4th row: P.13 n., 4 wh., 3 n., 4 wh., 13 n.
5th row: K.13 n., 2 wh., 1 n., 2 wh., 1 n., 2 wh., 1 n., 2 wh., 13 n.

When working the 6th row, join in a small ball of red wool on the 4th st. Weave for.1 st., then p. the "1 r.". Weave for 1 st., then drop the red thread. Join in the second red ball at the other side. Continue weaving the red threads as above for 1 st. on either side of the red stitches, until the 32nd row is reached.

6th row: P.5 n., 1 r., 7 n., 2 wh., 2 n., 3 wh., 2 n., 2 wh., 7 n., 1 r., 5 n.
7th row: K.6 n., 1 r., 1 n., 1 r., 4 n., 2 wh., 3 n., 1 wh., 3 n., 2 wh., 4 n., 1 r., 1 n., 1 r., 6 n.
8th row: P.7 n., 2 r., 1 n., 1 r., 2 n., 2 wh., 7 n., 2 wh., 2 n., 1 r., 1 n., 2 r., 7 n.
9th row: K.6 n., 3 r., 1 n., 1 r., 1 n., 1 r., 2 wh., 7 n., 2 wh., 1 r., 1 n., 1 r., 1 n., 3 r., 6 n.
10th row: P.9 n., 2 r., 1 n., 1 r., 2 wh., 7 n., 2 wh., 1 r., 1 n., 2 r., 9 n.
11th row: K.7 n., 4 r., 1 n., 1 r., 2 wh., 7 n., 2 wh., 1 r., 1 n., 4 r., 7 n.
12th row: P.11 n., 2 r., 2 wh., 7 n., 2 wh., 2 r., 11 n.
13th row: K.8 n., 5 r., 2 wh., 7 n., 2 wh., 5 r., 8 n.
14th row: P.13 wh., 1 r., 2 wh., 5 n., 2 wh., 1 r., 13 wh.
15th row: K.1 n., 13 wh., 1 r., 2 wh., 3 n., 2 wh., 1 r., 13 wh., 1 n.
16th row: P.2 n., 2 wh., 9 n., 2 wh., 1 r., 2 wh., 1 n., 2 wh., 1 r., 2 wh., 9 n., 2 wh., 2 n.
17th row: K.3 n., 2 wh., 9 n., 2 wh., 1 r., 3 wh., 1 r., 2 wh., 9 n., 2 wh., 3 n.
18th row: P.4 n., 2 wh., 9 n., 2 wh., 3 n., 2 wh., 9 n., 2 wh., 4 n.
19th row: K.5 n., 2 wh., 9 n., 1 wh., 1 n., 1 r., 1 n., 1 wh., 9 n., 2 wh., 5 n.
20th row: As 18th row.
21st row: As 17th row.
22nd row: As 16th row.
23rd row: As 15th row.
24th row: As 14th row.
25th row: As 13th row.
26th row: As 12th row.
27th row: As 11th row.
28th row: As 10th row.
29th row: As 9th row.
30th row: As 8th row.
31st row: As 7th row.
32nd row: As 6th row. Break off red.
33rd row: As 5th row.
34th row: As 4th row.
35th row: As 3rd row.
36th row: As 2nd row.
37th row: As 1st row. Break off white. Cont. in stst. in navy only.

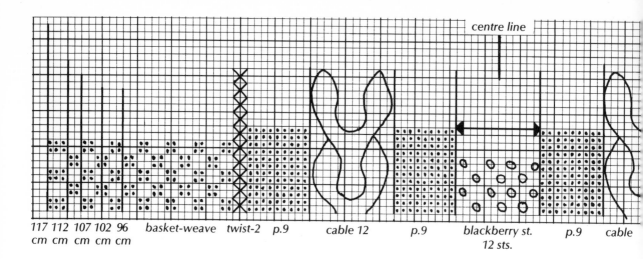

117 112 107 102 96   basket-weave   twist-2   p.9   cable 12   p.9   blackberry st.   p.9   cable
cm cm cm cm cm   12 sts.

"Bernard" (see plate 8)

A polo-necked Aran knit jersey based on the 96 cm
(38 in.) double-knit pattern. The Aran pattern can be
adapted for use on larger and smaller-sized garments (96-117 cm (38-46 in.) with the help of the following graph. This shows the placement of the Aran
panels and cables on the front and back of the garment with revised starting and finishing points for
the varying sizes.

    The basic instructions for the back in size 96 cm of
the raglan-sleeved pattern specify 105 stitches.
Because the "Bernard" pattern requires an even
number of stitches, 3 were added across the last row
of the ribbed band. (The extra 2 stitches compensate
for the elastic effect of the Aran panel.) Apply this
formula to whatever size has been chosen, casting
on the number of stitches specified and increasing
evenly over the last ribbed row to make up the number shown on the graph.

    After completing the ribbed band begin the Aran
pattern, or work 5 cm (2 in.) of the basket-weave

stitch across the entire width of the garment, if
preferred. (The basket-weave pattern could be re-
placed with moss stitch or garter stitch if desired.)

    The following gives row-by-row instructions for
the first Aran panel in the illustrated size. If you are
working a different size, simply adjust the number of
basket-weave stitches at each side. Remember to
keep the pattern set as the armhole and neck shapings are being made.

Abbreviations:
C.6b. (Cable 6 back): Sl. next 3 sts. onto cable needle.
Hold at back of work. K. next 3 sts., then k. the 3 sts.
from cable needle.
C.6f. (Cable 6 front): Sl. next 3 sts. onto cable needle.
Hold at front of work. K. next 3 sts., then k. the 3 sts.
from cable needle.
Tw.2 (Twist-2): K. into the front of the 2nd st. along l.h.
needle, then into the front of the 1st st., slipping both
loops off together.

Back and Front: Size 96 cm (38 in.).
After completing the band:

Pattern for sleeve

basket-weave   twist-2   p.7   cable 12   p.7   twist-2   basket-weave

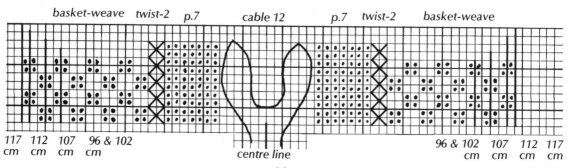

117 112 107 96 & 102   96 & 102 107 112 117
cm cm cm cm   centre line   cm cm cm cm

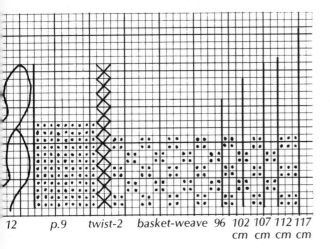

12 p.9 twist-2 basket-weave 96 102 107 112 117
cm cm cm cm

1st row: (K.2, p.2) 4 times, tw.2, p.9, k.12, p.30, k.12, p.9, tw.2, (p.2, k.2) 4 times.

2nd row: (P.2, k.2) 4 times, p.2, k.9, p.12, k.9, (p.3 tog., (k.1, p.1, k.1) into next st.) 3 times, k.9, p.12, k.9, p.2, (k.2, p.2) 4 times.

3rd row: (P.2, k.2) 4 times, tw.2, p.9, k.12, p.30, k.12, p.9, tw.2, (k.2, p.2) 4 times.

4th row: (K.2, p.2) 4 times, p.2, k.9, p.12, k.9, ((k.1, p.1, k.1) into next st., p.3 tog.) 3 times, k.9, p.12, k.9, p.2, (p.2, k.2) 4 times.

5th row: (K.2, p.2) 4 times, tw.2, p.9, c.6b., c.6f., p.30, c.6b., c.6f., p.9, tw.2, (p.2, k.2) 4 times.

6th row: (P.2, k.2) 4 times, p.2, k.9, p.12, k.9, (p.3 tog., (k.1, p.1, k.1) into next st.) 3 times, k.9, p.12, k.9, p.2, (k.2, p.2) 4 times.

7th row: (P.2, k.2) 4 times, tw.2, p.9, k.12, p.30, k.12, p.9, tw.2, (k.2, p.2) 4 times.

8th row: (K.2, p.2) 4 times, p.2, k.9, p.12, k.9, ((k.1, p.1, k.1) into next st., p.3 tog.) 3 times, k.9, p.12, k.9, p.2, (p.2, k.2) 4 times.

9th row: (K.2, p.2) 4 times, tw.2, p.9, k.12, p.30, k.12, p.9, tw.2, (p.2, k.2) 4 times.

10th row: (P.2, k.2) 4 times, p.2, k.9, p.12, k.9, (p.3 tog., (k.1, p.1, k.1) into next st.) 3 times, k.9, p.12, k.9, p.2, (k.2, p.2) 4 times.

11th row: (P.2, k.2) 4 times, tw.2, p.9, c.6b., c.6f., p.30, c.6b., c.6f., p.9, tw.2, (k.2, p.2) 4 times.

12th row: (K.2, p.2) 4 times, p.2, k.9, p.12, k.9, ((k.1, p.1, k.1) into next st., p.3 tog.) 3 times, k.9, p.12, k.9, p.2, (p.2, k.2) 4 times.

13th row: (K.2, p.2) 4 times, tw.2, p.9, k.12, p.30, k.12, p.9, tw.2, (p.2, k.2) 4 times.

14th row: (P.2, k.2) 4 times, p.2, k.9, p.12, k.9, (p.3 tog., (k.1, p.1, k.1) into next st.) 3 times, k.9, p.12, k.9, p.2, (k.2, p.2) 4 times.

15th row: (P.2, k.2) 4 times, tw.2, p.9, k.12, p.30, k.12, p.9, tw.2, (k.2, p.2) 4 times.

16th row: (K.2, p.2) 4 times, p.2, k.9, p.12, k.9, ((k.1, p.1, k.1) into next st., p.3 tog.) 3 times, k.9, p.12, k.9, p.2, (p.2, k.2) 4 times.

17th row: (K.2, p.2) 4 times, tw.2, p.9, c.6f., c.6b., p.30, c.6f., c.6b., p.9, tw.2, (p.2, k.2) 4 times.

18th row: (P.2, k.2) 4 times, p.2, k.9, p.12, k.9, (p.3 tog., (k.1, p.1, k.1) into next st.) 3 times, k.9, p.12, k.9, p.2, (k.2, p.2) 4 times.

19th row: (P.2, k.2) 4 times, tw.2, p.9, k.12, p.30, k.12, p.9, tw.2, (k.2, p.2) 4 times.

20th row: (K.2, p.2) 4 times, p.2, k.9, p.12, k.9, ((k.1, p.1, k.1) into next st., p.3 tog.) 3 times, k.9, p.12, k.9, p.2, (p.2, k.2) 4 times.

21st row: (K.2, p.2) 4 times, tw.2, p.9, k.12, p.30, k.12, p.9, tw.2, (p.2, k.2) 4 times.

22nd row: (P.2, k.2) 4 times, p.2, k.9, p.12, k.9, (p.3 tog., (k.1, p.1, k.1) into next st.) 3 times, k.9, p.12, k.9, p.2, (k.2, p.2) 4 times.

23rd row: (P.2, k.2) 4 times, tw.2, p.9, c.6f., c.6b., p.30, c.6f., c.6b., p.9, tw.2, (k.2, p.2) 4 times.

24th row: (K.2, p.2) 4 times, p.2, k.9, p.12, k.9, ((k.1, p.1, k.1) into next st., p.3 tog.) 3 times, k.9, p.12, k.9, p.2, (p.2, k.2) 4 times.

These 24 rows complete one pattern. Repeat them for the required length.

Sleeve: Size 96 cm (38 in.)
The sleeve requires an even number of stitches, so reduce one stitch for all sizes.

The following 8 rows set the pattern, which should now be quite familiar after working the back and front.

1st row: K.1, p.2, (k.2, p.2) twice, tw.2, p.7, k.12, p.7, tw.2, (p.2, k.2) twice, p.2, k.1.

2nd row: P.1, k.2, (p.2, k.2) twice, p.2, k.7, p.12, k.7, p.2, (k.2, p.2) twice, k.2, p.1.

3rd row: P.1, k.2, (p.2, k.2) twice, tw.2, p.7, k.12, p.7, tw.2, (k.2, p.2) twice, k.2, p.1.

4th row: (1st increase row) Inc. in 1st st., p.2, (k.2, p.2) twice, p.3, k.7, p.12, k.7, p.2, (p.2, k.2) twice, p.2, inc. in last st.

5th row: (K.2, p.2) 3 times, tw.2, p.7, c.6b., c.6f., p.7, tw.2, (p.2, k.2) 3 times.

6th row: (P.2, k.2) 3 times, p.2, k.7, p.12, k.7, p.2, (k.2, p.2) 3 times.

7th row: (P.2, k.2) 3 times, tw.2, p.7, k.12, p.7, tw.2, (k.2, p.2) 3 times.

8th row: (K.2, p.2) 3 times, p.2, k.7, p.12, k.7, p.2, (p.2, k.2) 3 times.

Continue thus, cabling on the 5th, 11th, 17th and 23rd rows of the 24-row cable pattern as shown for the front and back. The number of basket-weave stitches at the side will decrease as the sleeve shapings are made.

Variations on a theme (see plate 9)

The preceding examples demonstrate the tremendous versatility of knitting when basic shapes are used as a starting point for experimentation.

To carry the concept even further, consider the striped overblouse illustrated in plate 9. (This garment is knitted across from sleeve edge to sleeve edge; basic shaping instructions are given on page 39.)

By adjusting the pattern with any of the following variations the finished article could assume a totally different appearance:

1. It could be made into a thigh-length garment by adding approximately 20 stitches to those which are cast on for the side seams in the basic pattern.

2. It could be made into a long-sleeved garment by:
(a) Adding a further 20 cm (8 in.) into the sleeve length at the beginning and end of each section.
(b) Adding a further 15 cm (6 in.) into the sleeve length and knitting a 5 cm (2 in.) ribbed cuff, if a close-fitting wristband is preferred.

3. It could be knitted all in one colour.

4. There are many variations on the striped pattern but whatever series of stripes is adopted, these must be worked in reverse order once the centre-front is reached. There are many more possibilities. Here are just a few variations!

(a) A set of contrasting stripes each side of the centre-front which is repeated on the sleeves.

(b) The same garment with armhole stripes, giving a blouse and jerkin effect.

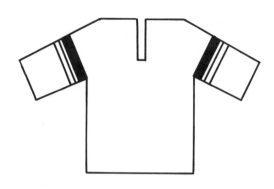

(c) Striped sleeves, plain side-fronts with the sleeve pattern repeated on the centre-front.

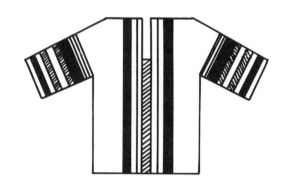

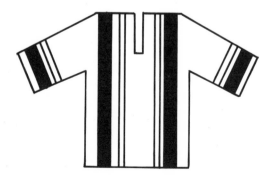

5. The illustrated garment is knitted in garter stitch. The following stitch variations could be made:
(a) Use stocking stitch stripes throughout.
(b) Knit the garment in one colour only with "self-stripes" of garter stitch or moss stitch.
(c) Knit garter stitch or reverse stocking stitch stripes with the main body of the garment in stocking stitch. This gives the appearance of Mexican woven cloth as the stripes are merged and not so harshly defined.

(d) The illustrated garment could be turned inside out and, indeed, the author found it hard to decide which way it should actually be worn.

6. The neck edging and centre-front opening:

(a) Could be faced with crochet, with or without a picot edging.

(b) Could have a garter stitch or k.1, p.1 ribbed edging.

(c) Either of the above variations could be finished at the neck edge with a long rope twist tied into a bow.

(d) Two frogs and a wooden toggle could provide the finishing.

(e) The neck opening could have been eliminated altogether, and the stitches picked up for a polo neck.

7. The sleeve and lower hem trim could have been:

(a) Knitted in a k.1, p.1 (or k.2, p.2) rib.

(b) Finished with crochet.

(c) Thickly fringed.

No doubt many more variations have suggested themselves as you have read through this section. All should be workable provided that sufficient time is taken to graph or design the pattern before the garment is begun.

"Juanita"

Basic shaping instructions for the overblouse illustrated in plate 9. The illustrated sample (size 91 cm) used fourteen 50-gram balls of double-knitting wool (five cream, four tan and five brown). The optional, thick cord-twist tie belt requires an extra ball of wool. Use fourteen 6-metre lengths of wool and follow the instructions for the rope twist.

Tension: 9½ sts. and 8 rows to 5 cm (5 sts. and 4 rows to 1 in.) over garter st.

The garment is knitted across from sleeve edge to sleeve edge in double-knitting wool on 4 mm needles. The neck opening and hems may be worked in picot or rib. Instructions are given for both.

Bust size:	81	86	91	96	cm.
	32	34	36	38	in.

Front:
Comm. at
sleeve edge by
casting on | 40 | 42 | 42 | 44 | sts.,
and k. in garter | 17.5 | 17.5 | 20 | 20 | st. for cm.
| | 7 | 7 | 8 | 8 | in. **
R.s.f., inc. 1 st. at
beg. of next
row. (This inc.
edge now
becomes
underarm edge
of work.) Inc.
1 st. at this edge
on foll. | 9 | 11 | 11 | 13 | rows.
At beg. of next
underarm edge
row, cast on
loosely | 54 | 56 | 58 | 58 | sts.
| (104 | 110 | 112 | 116 | sts.)
Cont. straight
until work
measures | 12 | 13 | 14 | 15.5 | cm
| 4¾ | 5 | 5¼ | 6 | in.
from side seam.
At neck edge,
dec. 1 st. on alt.
rows until | 99 | 104 | 106 | 109 | sts. rem.
Tie in a contrast
thread at neck
edge. Cont.,
dec. 1 st. on alt.
rows until | 95 | 99 | 101 | 103 | sts. rem.

(continued)

| Bust size: | 81 | 86 | 91 | 96 | cm. |
	32	34	36	38	in.

Cont. straight until work measures

| | 20.75 | 22 | 23.25 | 24.5 | cm |
| | 8¼ | 8¾ | 9¼ | 9¾ | in. |

from side seam.

Neck opening:
At neck edge, cast off

| | 33 | 33 | 33 | 33 | sts. |

K. to end of row.
(If working in stripes, join in main colour.)
Cont. straight for

| | 3 | 3 | 3 | 3 | cm. |
| | 1¼ | 1¼ | 1¼ | 1¼ | in. |

Join in colour of previous contrast stripe and work 1 row.

Next row: Cast on

| | 33 | 33 | 33 | 33 | sts. |

for other side of neck-opening.
Now reverse order of stripes so both side fronts will match.
Cont. straight until work matches first side neck-opening to beg. of neck shapings.
Inc. 6 st. at neck-edge on alt. rows until there are

| | 99 | 104 | 106 | 109 | sts. |

on the needle.
Tie in a second contrast thread at neck-edge.
Cont. inc. 1 st. at neck-edge on alt. rows until there are

| | 104 | 110 | 112 | 116 | sts. |

Cont. straight until work measures

| | 44.5 | 47 | 49.5 | 52 | cm |
| | 17½ | 18¼ | 19½ | 20½ | in. |

| Bust size: | 81 | 86 | 91 | 96 | cm. |
	32	34	36	38	in.

from side seam.
At side seam edge, cast off for the opposite side seam, then dec. 1 st. at underarm edge on next

	54	56	58	58	sts.
	10	12	12	14	rows.
(	40	42	42	44	sts.)

Cont. straight for

| | 17.5 | 17.5 | 20 | 20 | cm. |
| | 7 | 7 | 8 | 8 | in. |

Back:
Work as front to **.
R.s.f., inc. 1 st. at end of next row.
(This inc. edge now becomes the underarm edge of work.)
Inc. 1 st. at this edge on foll.

| | 9 | 11 | 11 | 13 | rows. |

At beg. of next underarm edge row cast on loosely

| | 54 | 56 | 58 | 58 | sts. |
| (104 | 110 | 112 | 116 | sts.) |

Cont. straight until work measures

| | 12 | 13 | 14 | 15.5 | cm |
| | 4¾ | .5 | 5¼ | 6 | in. |

from side seam.
At neck-edge, dec. 1 st. at beg. of every alt. row until

| | 99 | 104 | 106 | 109 | sts. rem. |

Tie in a contrast thread at neck-edge.
Cont. straight across back neck, matching stripes to those of front (if applicable) until work reaches the 2nd coloured marker placed on the front.
At neck-edge, inc. 1 st. on alt.

Bust size:	81	86	91	96	cm.
	32	34	36	38	in.

rows until there
are **104 110 112 116 sts.**
on the needle.
Cont. straight
until work
measures **44.5 47 49.5 52 cm**
17½ 18¼ 19½ 20½ in.
from side seam.
At underarm
edge cast off **54 56 58 58 sts.**
for opposite
side seam, then
dec. 1 st. at
underarm edge
on next **10 12 12 14 rows.**
(**40 42 42 44 sts.)**
Cont. straight
for a further **17.5 17.5 20 20 cm.**
7 7 8 8 in.
Cast off.

Picot trim:
Sew along
shoulder and
top sleeve
seams. With
4 mm needles
and r.s.f., join in
wool at lower
edge of right
side of neck
opening.
Pick up and k. **32 32 32 32 sts.**
up neck
opening, and **34 36 40 44 sts.**
around neck
and across to
centre-back
neck. (**66 68 70 76 sts.)**

All sizes:
1st row: P.
2nd row: K.32, k.2 tog.,
k. to end.
3rd row: P.
Rept. last 2 rows once.
6th row: K.1, (wl.fwd.,
k.2 tog.) to last st., k.1.
7th row: P.
8th row: K.32, inc. in
next st., k. to end.
9th row: P.
Rept. last 2 rows once.

Cast off loosely,
using a size
larger needle.
Now join in the
wool at the
centre-back
neck and, with
r.s.f., pick up
and k. **34 36 40 44 sts.**
across the
remainder of
the back and
side neck, and
32 sts. (all sizes)
down the left
edge of the
front opening.
1st row: P.32, p.2 tog.,
p. to end.
2nd row: K.
Rept. these 2 rows
once.
5th row: P.
6th row: K.1 (wl.fwd.,
k.2 tog.) to last st., k.1.
7th row: P.
8th row: K.
9th row: P.32, inc. in
next st., p. to end.
Rept. last 2 rows once.
Cast off loosely, using a
size larger needle.

Picot sleeve edges:
Pick up and k. **68 70 72 76 sts.**
across sleeve
edges.
Commencing
with a p. row,
work 5 rows stst.
6th row: K.1
(wl.fwd.,
k.2 tog.) to last
st., k.1.
Work a further
5 rows stst.
Cast off loosely,
using a size
larger needle.

*Picot trim, front
and back hems:*
Pick up and k. **104 110 116 122 sts.**

41

Bust size:	81	86	91	96	cm.
	32	34	36	38	in.

across lower
edge.
Complete picot
trim as for
sleeves.
Press picot
edgings open.
With r.s.f.,
neatly oversew
the two
neckband
sections at the
centre-back
neck. Fold the
edging in half
along the row of
holes and
slip-stitch
loosely into
place on the
inside.
Slip-stitch picot
edging to
centre-front
opening base.

Ribbed edgings
(1 × 1 or 2 × 2
rib):

Neck-band:
Sew along
shoulder and
top sleeve
seams. With
4 mm needles
and r.s.f., join in
wool at top of
right side of
neck-opening.

Bust size:	81	86	91	96	cm.
Pick up and k.	68	72	80	88	sts.

around neck
and across
back-neck to
top of left side
of
neck-opening.
Work 6 rows in
rib.
Cast off loosely
ribwise.
Join wool to
lower edge of

right side of
neck opening.
Pick up and k.
(all sizes) 36 sts.
up side of neck
opening plus
the edge of
neck ribbing.
Work 6 rows in
rib. Cast off
ribwise.
Join wool to
opposite side of
neck opening
and complete to
match. On the
inside, catch
ribbed trim
neatly to the
base of the neck
opening.

*Sleeves and front and
back hems:*
Pick up and k. the
number of sts. specified
for the picot trim, and
work 6 rows in rib. Cast
off loosely ribwise.

The rope twist:
Knot three 120 cm. (60 in.) strands of wool together
at each end. Anchor one end securely over a cupboard handle or under a chair leg. Stand back,
stretching the strands taut. Place a finger inside the
knot at the far end and commence turning the wool
in a clockwise direction until the tightly-twisted wool
starts winding back on itself when the pressure is
relaxed slightly. Place a finger in the middle of the
wool twist and, holding the two knotted ends firmly
together, release the anchored end. The wool will
"jump" into a twist. Run it through the hands to even
out the rope. This wool twist will never unravel. Tie a
fresh knot near the end and tassel the short end
strands, or sew pompoms securely through the end
knots.

For a thicker rope, use six strands of wool.

Ski wear (see plate 10)

A selection of basic hat, mitten and scarf patterns which, although not strictly variations on the basic patterns, are sufficiently general to be used as a basis for original designs. These articles can be made for winter warmth for anyone in cold climates and the patterns can be adapted to suit a variety of sizes.

Ski-hat: Patterns are given for ladies' and men's sizes. Because head sizes are fairly general the ladies' size will fit a child. For a toddler the turn-up can be doubled over or rolled up to suit.

Scarf: The ladies' and children's patterns are simply variations on the basic men's scarf pattern.

Mittens: Men's and ladies' ski mittens which can be worked with or without the snowflake motif in the illustration.

Materials:

Ladies' ski hat, mittens and one-colour scarf: Twelve 25-gram balls or six 50-gram balls (11 oz.) main colour and one 25-gram ball (½ oz.) contrast colour (if working the snowflake motif).

Men's ski hat, mittens and two-colour scarf: Twelve 25-gram balls or six 50-gram balls (10 oz.) main colour, four 25-gram balls or two 50-gram balls (3 oz.) contrast colour.

Ski mittens

Instructions are given here for the men's and ladies' sizes together. Simply read across the column from left to right and take the figures given for appropriate size.

Top:	Men's	Ladies'	
Using 3¼ mm needles and white wool, cast on	23	21	sts.
Work in 1 × 1 rib for	10	7.5	cm.
	4	3	in.

Change to 4 mm needles:
Inc. 1 st. at each end 1st row, *work 16 rows stst. (25   23   sts.)
Join in orange wool and work the 19 rows of the snowflake motif (see next page). Break off orange.
**36th row: P.2 tog. p. each end of row.
37th row: Cont. in stst. and dec. 1 st. each end of row.
38th row: Work without shaping.
39th row: Work without shaping.

Rept. these 3 rows until 9 sts. remain.   Work 1 row.   Cast off.
Cast off.

*If omitting the snowflake motif, work 35 rows stst., then from ** to end.

Underside:
Using 3¼ mm needles and white wool, cast on   21   19   sts.
Change to 4 mm needles.
Work in 1 × 1 rib to match the mitten top.
Break off white. Cont. in stst. in orange wool.
Work 39 rows.
40th row: Dec. 1 st. at each end of row.
41st row: Work without shaping.
42nd row: Work without shaping.
Rept. these 3 rows until 9 sts. remain.   Work 2 rows.   Cast off.
Cast off.

Pin out and press on wrong sides over a damp cloth.
Thumb: (All sizes)
Using 3¼ mm needles, cast on 2 sts.
1st row: Inc. 1 st. each end of row.
2nd row: P.
3rd row: K.
4th row: P.
Rept. these 4 rows until there are 16 sts.
Work 9 rows stst.
Commence shaping:
1st row: K.2 tog. each end of row.
2nd row: P.
3rd row: K.
4th row: P.
Rept. these 4 rows once (12 sts.). Break wool off about 30 cm (12 in.) from work. Thread the wool onto a sewing needle, pass through the remaining 12 sts. and draw up firmly, securing with a few overstitches. Sew down the

thumb seam until the gusset shapings are reached. Press the thumb and thumb seam. Turn right side out. Place the thumb so that the point of the gusset is level with the top of the wrist band. Pin in place and crochet (or blanket stitch) the thumb and gusset into place. Continue stitching around the mitten on the outside of the work so that the edging forms a contrasting welt on the right side of the work.

Snowflake motif

motif
19 sts. wide

ladies
men

Abbreviations: wh., white; or., orange.

Instructions are given here for the men's ski mittens with figures for the ladies' ski mittens in brackets.

1st row: K.6 (5) wh., 2 or., 9 wh., 2 or., 6 (5) wh.
2nd row: P.6 (5) wh., 3 or., 7 wh., 3 or., 6 (5) wh.
3rd row: K.6 (5) wh., 4 or., 5 wh., 4 or., 6 (5) wh.
4th row: P.3 (2) wh., 3 or., 1 wh., 4 or., 3 wh., 4 or., 1 wh., 3 or., 3 (2) wh.
5th row: K.3 (2) wh., (4 or., 1 wh.) 3 times, 4 or., 3 (2) wh.

6th row: P.4 (3) wh., 4 or., 1 wh., (3 or., 1 wh.) twice, 4 or., 4 (3) wh.
7th row: K.5 (4) wh., 4 or., 1 wh., (2 or., 1 wh.) twice, 4 or., 5 (4) wh.
8th row: P.6 (5) wh., 4 or., (1 wh., 1 or.) twice, 1 wh., 4 or., 6 (5) wh.
9th row: K.7 (6) wh., 4 or., 3 wh., 4 or., 7 (6) wh.
10th row: Break off or. P. in wh. Join in or.
11th row: As 9th row.
12th row: As 8th row.
13th row: As 7th row.
14th row: As 6th row.
15th row: As 5th row.
16th row: As 4th row.
17th row: As 3rd row.
18th row: As 2nd row.
19th row: As 1st row. Break off or.

Men's ski hat

Abbreviations: wh., white; or., orange.

Using orange wool and 3¼ mm needles, cast on 149 sts. Work 2 rows 1 × 1 rib (k.1, p.1). Change to 4 mm needles. Using the Fair Isle motif from the mitten pattern, but reversing the colours, proceed as follows:
1st row: Rib 63 or., join in wh., and work the 1st row of the snowflake motif in stst. over next 21 sts. Mark each side of this Fair Isle panel with a contrast thread for reference. Drop the wh. thread, rib 63 or.
Cont. until the snowflake motif is completed. Break off white.
Next row: Rib 63, k.23, rib 63.
Cont. in rib until the work measures 22.5 cm (9 in.). W.s.f.
1st row: K.2 *(p.1, k.1) 3 times, p.1, sl.1, k.1, p.s.s.o., k.1, k.2 tog., (p.1, k.1) 3 times, k.1. Rept. from * to last 3 sts., rib 3.
2nd row: Rib 3, *(p.1, k.1) 3 times, p.3, k.1, (p.1, k.1) 3 times. Rept. from * to last 3 sts., rib 3.
3rd row: K.2, *(p.1, k.1) 3 times, p.1, k.3, (p.1, k.1) 3 times. Rept. from * to last 3 sts., rib 3.
4th row: As 2nd row to last 3 sts., rib 3.
5th row: K.2, *(p.1, k.1) 3 times, p.1, k.3 tog. t.b.l., (p.1, k.1) 3 times. Rept. from * to last 3 sts., rib 3.
6th-8th rows: Rib.
9th row: K.2, *(p.1, k.1) twice, p.1, sl.1, k.1, p.s.s.o., k.1, k.2 tog., (p.1, k.1) twice. Rept. from * to last 3 sts., rib 3.
10th row: Rib 3, *(p.1, k.1) twice, p.3, k.1, (p.1, k.1) twice. Rept. from * to last 2 sts., rib 2.
11th row: K.2, *(p.1, k.1) twice, p.1, k.3, (p.1, k.1) twice. Rept. from * to last 3 sts., rib 3.
12th row: As 10th row.
13th row: K.2, *(p.1, k.1) twice, p.1, k.3 tog. t.b.l., (p.1,

k.1) twice. Rept. from * to last 3 sts., rib 3.
14th row: Rib.
15th row: K.2 tog., (p.1, k.1) twice, *k.3 tog. t.b.l., k.1, (p.1, k.1) 3 times. Rept. from * to last 9 sts., k.3 tog. t.b.l., (k.1, p.1) twice, p.2 tog.
16th row: K.2, p.1, k.1, *p.3, k.1, (p.1, k.1) twice. Rept. from * to last 7 sts., p.3, (k.1, p.1) twice.
17th row: P.2 tog., k.1, p.1, *k.3 tog. t.b.l., p.1, (k.1, p.1) twice. Rept. from * to last 7 sts., k.3 tog. t.b.l., p.1, k.1, p.2 tog.
18th row: Rib.
19th row: K.2, *k.3 tog. t.b.l., k.1, p.1, k.1. Rept from * to last 5 sts., k.3 tog. t.b.l., k.1, p.1.
20th row: K.1, (p.3, k.1) to end.
21st row: K.1, (k.2 tog.) to end.

Break wool 1 metre from work. Thread on to sewing needle and run through the stitches, drawing them up tightly and securing with a few overstitches. With the same thread, join the back seam of the hat using a flat overstitch seam. Note that the snowflake motif will be facing right side out during seaming. Turn the hat inside out and carefully press the motif only. Do not press any of the ribbing. Turn up the band so that the snowflake motif is at centre front with two rows of the orange ribbing showing beneath it. Catch the band in place with a few stitches if necessary. These can be removed for washing or drying the hat.

Ladies' and children's ski hat

This pattern does not include the snowflake motif because the turn-up on the hat is not sufficiently wide to accommodate it.

Using 3$\frac{1}{4}$ mm needles and main-colour wool, cast on 129 sts. Work 2 rows 1 × 1 rib, then change to 4 mm needles. Cont. in rib until the work measures 16.5 cm (6$\frac{1}{2}$ in.) from the beginning.

Commence shaping:
1st row: K.1, *(p.1, k.1) 3 times, p.1, sl.1, k.1, p.s.s.o., k.1, k.2 tog., (p.1, k.1) twice. Rept. from * to end.
2nd row: *(P.1, k.1) twice, p.3, k.1, (p.1, k.1) 3 times. Rept. from * to last st., p.1.
3rd row: K.1, *(p.1, k.1) 3 times, p.1, k.3, (p.1, k.1) twice. Rept. from * to end.
4th row: As 2nd row.
5th row: K.1, *(p.1, k.1) 3 times, p.1, k.3 tog. t.b.l., (p.1, k.1) twice. Rept. from * to end.
6th-8th rows: Rib.
9th row: K.1, *(p.1, k.1) twice, p.1, sl.1, k.1, p.s.s.o., k.1, k.2 tog., p.1, k.1. Rept. from * to end.
10th row: P.1, k.1, p.3, k.1, (p.1, k.1) twice. Rept. from * to last st., p.1.
11th row: K.1, *(p.1, k.1) twice, p.1, k.3, p.1, k.1. Rept. from * to end.

12th row: As 10th row.
13th row: K.1, *(p.1, k.1) twice, p.1, k.3 tog. t.b.l., p.1, k.1. Rept. from * to end. (65 sts.)
14th row: P.1, (k.1, p.1) to end.
15th row: K.1, *(p.1, k.1) twice, k.3 tog. t.b.l., k.1. Rept. from * to end.
16th row: *P.3, k.1, p.1, k.1. Rept. from * to last st., p.1. (49 sts.)
17th row: K.1, *p.1, k.1, p.1, k.3 tog. t.b.l. Rept. from * to end. (33 sts.)
18th row: P.1, (k.1, p.1) to end.

Break wool 1 metre from work. Thread on to a sewing needle and run the wool through the stitches, drawing them up tightly and securing with a few overstitches. With the same thread, join the back seam of the hat using a flat overstitch seam. Turn the hat inside out. Do not press. Turn up the band and catch in place with a few stitches if necessary. These can be removed for washing or drying the hat.

Men's scarf

Abbreviations: wh., white; or., orange.

Using orange wool and 4 mm needles, cast on 51 sts. Set rib as follows:
1st row: K.2, (p.1, k.1) to last 2 sts., k.2.
2nd row: Sl.1, (p.1, k.1) to end of row. Rept. these 2 rows once more.
Cont., keeping a 5-st. ribbed border on each side, *working the centre panel in stst. until the work measures 10 cm (4 in.).
Next row: Rib 5, k.11, place the contrast thread to mark the perimeter of the snowflake motif, join in wh. and work 1st row of motif as follows:
K.3 or., 2 wh., 9 or., 2 wh., 3 or., (drop wh.) put 2nd marker in place, k.11 or., rib 5. Cont. until snowflake motif has been completed. Break off wh. Cont. in or. until scarf measures 127 cm (50 in.). Work right across in rib for 4 rows. Cast off. Press.

Cut lengths of wh. wool 20 cm (8 in.) long. With a crochet hook and 3 strands of wool, make a fringe along each end.

Ladies' scarf

Work as for men's scarf until *. Work the centre panel in stst. until work measures 122 cm (48 in.). **Work right across in rib for 4 rows. Cast off. Press. Pleat each end of scarf and overstitch securely. Make two pompoms and attach one to each end of scarf.**

Children's scarf

Work as for man's scarf until *. Work the centre panel in stst. until work measures 100 cm (39$\frac{1}{2}$ in.). Cont. as for ladies' scarf from ** to **.

4-ply

Using 4-ply

The 4-ply charts at the back of this book cover the same garments that are illustrated in the double-knitting section. These can all be hand- or machine-knitted. To make one of the illustrated garments in 4-ply, simply substitute the appropriate needles and instructions. Remember, however, that 4-ply, being finer and worked on smaller needles, will produce a smaller Fair Isle motif, fancy panel stitch or Aran cable than double-knitting wool. For this reason it is often preferred for babies' and toddlers' wear. It is also suitable for adults' fashion garments. (See illustration of v-necked tunic in plate 11. This garment was worked entirely in stocking stitch with 1 × 1 ribbed cuffs, bands and a v-neck. The stripes alone transform it from a plain, uninteresting top into a fashion garment.)

Four-ply is also an ideal weight for summer and evening wear, and it lends itself beautifully to the finest of lacy stitches. It is therefore a much more versatile wool than double-knit, and, for professional results, is well worth the extra time involved in knitting.

The following pages give instructions for a selection of miscellaneous 4-ply items in addition to information on basic pattern conversions.

Belted jackets and jerkins

The 4-ply v-neck and basic cardigan patterns can easily be adapted to make thigh-length, sleeveless or long-sleeved jackets and jerkins. If a pattern is being extended to make a jacket or jerkin with long sleeves, allow one extra 50-gram ball of wool for sizes 61-86 cm (24-34 in.) and two 50-gram balls for sizes 91-117 cm (36-46 in.).

If knitting a sleeveless version of any basic pattern, deduct one 50-gram ball from the quantities given for a long-sleeved garment for small sizes and two 50-gram balls for larger sizes. Use the armband pattern given for the sleeveless v-necked jumper. These calculations should include sufficient wool for a plain belt and crocheted or plaited belt loops. (Instructions below.)

To lengthen the basic pattern: Commence at the lower edge of the back and front(s). Using 3¼ mm needles, cast on the required number of sts. Work 6 rows in rib or a full ribbed band if preferred. Change to 3¾ mm needles and commence the main pattern, working an extra 6.5-7 cm (2½-3 in.) for all sizes up to 71 cm (28 in.) chest. For sizes 76-117 cm (30-46 in.) add an extra 10-12.75 cm (4-5 in.). Change back to

3¼ mm needles and continue in pattern to armhole, adding the extra length to the instructions.

Belt: Using 2¾ mm needles, cast on 12 sts. and rib to match the bands for the length required.

Belt with buckle or dome fasteners: Work for waist measurement plus 10 cm (4 in.).

Tie-belt: (Allow one extra 50-gram ball for the tie-belt.) Work for waist measurement, plus 102 cm (40 in.) for small and medium sizes or 122 cm (48 in.) for larger sizes.

Belt loops: Crochet, plait or knit these and fix them firmly at the waistline of the garment.

Knitted belt loops: Using 2¾ mm needles, cast on 5 sts. and rib as follows:
1st row: Sl.1, (k.1, p.1) twice.
2nd row: Sl.1, (p.1, k.1) twice for 4 cm (1½ in.).

Knitted belt loops can be made a feature of the garment if a set of six are made and placed at the side seams, centre-side fronts, and centre-side backs.

A variation on the basic 4-ply pattern

"Clare" (see plate 11)

This v-necked tunic can be adapted from the basic 4-ply pattern in the desired size with the alterations outlined below. It is worked mainly in stocking stitch with 1 × 1 ribbed cuffs and bands; the main body, sleeves and belt are worked in white, and a striped pattern of dark and pale-blue denim appears on the back, front and sleeves.

Turn to the basic v-necked jumper pattern in the correct size. Rib the 14 band and cuff rows in dark blue.

Change to 3¼ mm needles and inc. the 6 sts. mentioned in the instructions evenly across the 1st stst. row of the front and back. Work the striped pattern in stst. as follows:
20 rows dark blue
14 rows pale blue
14 rows dark blue
6 rows pale blue
6 rows dark blue
2 rows pale blue
2 rows dark blue.

Change to white wool, and continue to follow the basic instructions, working the extra back and front length suggested for a tunic before shaping the armholes.

Sleeves: Work as outlined in the basic instructions, including the striped pattern, as above.

Lacy stole or fashion scarf (see plates 12 and 13)

Use 4-ply wool doubled throughout.

Materials: Ten 25-gram balls or five 50-gram balls (8 oz.) of 4-ply wool.

Measurements:
Length: 152 cm (60 in.)
Width: 46 cm (18 in.)

Using 6½ mm needles, cast on 44 sts.
1st row: K.1, (k.1, winding the wool around the needle twice) to last st., k.1.
2nd row: K.1, (k. into the first loop of the next st., then sl. both loops off the needle together, forming 1 long st.) to last st., k.1.

Rept. these 2 rows 95 times, then the 1st row once. Cast off, knitting into 1st loop as before.

Press very lightly over a damp cloth.

Fringe: Cut 6 pieces of wool 35.5 cm (14 in.) long and fold in half. Draw the looped end through 1st cast-on stitch with a crochet hook. Pull the cut ends through the loop and pull the ends tight. Cont. thus along each end of the scarf, giving a total of 88 fringe tassels.

Hot water bottle cover (see plate 14)

Materials: Five 25-gram balls or three 50-gram balls (4 oz.) of 4-ply wool.

Using 2¾ mm needles, cast on 62 sts. and work in k.1, p.1 rib for 7.5 cm (3 in.).
Threading row: (Rib 2, wl.fwd., k.2 tog.) to last 2 sts., rib 2. Work a further 5 rows in rib.
Change to 3¼ mm needles:
1st row: P.2, (k.3, p.2) to end.
2nd row: K.2, (p.3, k.2) to end.
Cont. straight in ribbed pattern until the work measures 32 cm (12½ in.) or reaches to the base of an existing hot-water bottle when the threading row is held around the base of the bottle neck. Form the base opening for the hanging tab thus:
Next row: Keeping the ribbed pattern correct, work 23 sts., cast off next 16 sts. and pattern to end.
Next row: Pattern for 23 sts., cast on 16 sts., pattern to end. Cont. in the pattern or plain stst. for the underside until the work matches the front of the cover to the base of the ribbing. Change to 2¾ mm needles and work 5 rows in rib. Work another threading row as above. Cont. in rib for another 7.5 cm (3 in.). Cast off ribwise. Join the ribbed tops with a neat, flat overstitch and the body of the cover with back stitch. Make a tasselled wool twist, thread through the holes and tie with a bow. Hot water bottle covers (with or without the hot water bottle) make an unusual gift.

Adult's bed sox (see plate 14)

Materials: One pair of 4½ mm needles and four 25-gram or two 50-gram (3 oz.) balls of 4-ply.

The sox are worked in garter stitch (all rows k.) with ribbed cuffs. Read across instructions from left to right.

	Small to medium foot	Large or long foot	
Cast on	82	94	sts.
K. 1 row.			
Inc. in 1st st. on every row until there are	96	108	sts.
Cont. straight until work measures 6 cm (2¼ in.).			
Dec. 1 st. at beg. of every row until there are	82	94	sts.
Cast off	18	22	sts.
at beg. of next 2 rows.			
Work 8 rows on the remaining	46	50	sts.
Work 4 rows in k.2, p.2 rib.			

Threading row: (K.2, wl.fwd., k.2 tog.) to last 2 sts., k.2. Rib a further 9 rows. Cast off ribwise.
Make a wool twist, or thread a ribbon through the slots, finishing with a bow.

Child's slippers (see plate 14)

Measurements: To fit child's foot 15-18 cm (6-7 in.) long.

Materials: Two 50-gram balls (3 oz.) of thick double-knitting wool, or the same amount of 4-ply wool used double. One pair of 3¼ mm needles.

Cast on 42 sts. and work 30 rows garter st. (all rows k.).
Cast off loosely 10 sts. at beg. of next 2 rows.
Work 24 rows on remaining 22 sts.
Next row: K.2 tog. all along row.
Next row: K.
Next row: K.1, (k.2 tog.) to end. (6 sts.)
Next row: K.
Moss st. 26 rows on these 6 sts., then work 6 rows garter st. Cast off.

Bring moss st. instep strip up along the front of the slipper so that the cast-off edge is 2.5 cm (1 in.) from the top.

With r.s.f. and using a neat overstitch on the outside of the work, sew the moss st. strip to the foot of the slipper. Oversew the back heel seam. Catch the front flaps back and finish each with a button or an embroidered flower.

Garden tea cosy (see plate 14)

Materials: Six 25-gram balls or three 50-gram balls (5 oz.) double-knitting wool plus an assortment of coloured scraps. Double-knitting wool should be used throughout, or 3 strands of 4-ply can be used.

The cosy is worked throughout in fisherman's rib. It is useful to remember when counting rows in this stitch, that there are two rows to each "hole" in the knitting.

Using 4 mm needles, cast on 33 sts.
1st row: K.2, (p.1, k.1) to last st., k.1.
2nd row: K.1, (p.1, k. into the base of next st. (actually the previous row) slipping all loops, including the st. on l.h. needle, off together) to last 2 sts., p.1, k.1.
3rd row: K.1, (k. into the row below, p.1) to last st., k.1.
4th row: As 2nd row.
Cont. in this rib, working every k. st. into the row below, until 56 rows have been completed. (These will count as 28 rows of stst.)
Next row: K.1 (k.3 tog., p.1) to last 4 sts., k.3 tog., k.1.
Fisherman's rib for 5 rows.
Next row: As previous dec. row.
Cast off in rib. Work another identical piece.

Sew up the two halves using a neat, flat overstitch. On one seam, stitch for 2.5 cm (1 in.), leaving 6.5 cm (2½ in.) open for the teapot spout. On the remaining seam leave 10 cm (4 in.) open for the handle. Leave a round hole at the top for the knob on the teapot lid. Make 15 flowers, using scraps of brightly-coloured wool. Wind the wool around two fingers approximately 25 times. Remove the fingers, press flat and wind the wool around the centre 12 times. Cut the thread approximately 20 cm (8 in.) from the flower. Thread the end through a sewing needle and pass through the centre binding several times to secure. Leave the excess thread until required.

Using green wool, crochet a chain "stem" and "leaves" as follows: *Single chain 15, make "leaf" by looping chain and securing with a slip-stitch 5 links back, make 10 single chain, pick up the first flower by crocheting through the backs of the binding loops and secure to the cosy with a slip-stitch. Cont. from * working flowers around the top opening of the cosy (to cover the hole) and then for another row below. Finish by stitching excess wool securely to the cosy.

3-ply

Basic bootee and mitten patterns (see plate 15)

Bootees are a traditional gift, and no baby can have too many pairs. With this in mind, the following basic pattern was developed together with a basic mitten design. These can be used together to produce matching sets (a number of the author's variations are given) or they can provide a guide for original designs.

Materials: Two 25-gram balls (1 oz.) 3-ply baby wool or two 25-gram balls or one 50-gram ball for a matching set of bootees and mittens. Use 2¾ mm needles throughout.

Basic bootee pattern

Cast on 43 sts. K. 1 row.
1st row: K.1, inc. in next st., k.18, inc. in next st., k.1, inc. in next st., k.18, inc. in next st., k.1.
2nd & every alt. row: K.
3rd row: K.1, inc. in next st., k.20, inc. in next st., k.1, inc. in next st., k.20, inc. in next st., k.1.
Cont. thus, knitting 22, then 24, then 26 sts. between increases.
Next row: K.1, inc. in next st., k.28, inc. in next st., k.1, inc. in next st., k.28, inc. in next st., k.1. (67 sts.)
K. 10 rows garter st.
Shape for instep: K.39, k.2 tog., turn work, sl.1 (knitwise), p.11, p.2 tog., turn work. Cont. in stst. on these central sts., dec. at end of each row until there are 44 sts. left on the needles. K. to the end.
Work 3 rows stst. commencing with a p. row.
Threading row: K.1, *wl.fwd., k.2 tog. Rept. from * to last st., k.1.
Next row: P.
Next row: K.4, inc., *k.6, inc. Rept. from * to last 4 sts., k.4. (50 sts.)
(N.B. Pink pattern only: inc. in last st. of previous row. (51 sts.))
Next row: P. (Pink pattern only: k. this row.)
   Now commence the pattern of your choice from the following examples or substitute an original design.

Basic mitten pattern

Cast on 18 sts.
1st row: *K.3, inc., k.1, inc. Rept. from * to end of row. (24 sts.)
2nd & every alt. row: P.
3rd row: *K.4, inc., k.2, inc. Rept. from * to end of row. (30 sts.)

5th row: *K.5, inc., k.3, inc. Rept. from * to end of row. (36 sts.)
7th row: *K.6, inc., k.4, inc. Rept. from * to end of row. (42 sts.)
8th row: P.
Work 28 rows stst.
Threading row: K.1, *wl.fwd., k.2 tog. Rept. from * to last st., K.1.
Next row: P.
Next row: K.3, *inc., k.4. Rept. from * to last 3 sts., k.3. (50 sts.)
(N.B. Pink pattern only: inc. in last st. of previous row. (51 sts.))
Next row: P. (Pink pattern only: k. this row).
   Now commence the pattern of your choice or substitute an original design.

Pink pattern

1st row: K.1, *wl.fwd., k.3, k.3 tog., k.3, wl.fwd., k.1. Rept. from * to end of row.
2nd row: P.
3rd row: As 1st row.
4th row: K.
Rept. these 4 rows twice. Cast off loosely.

White pattern

Work 6 rows stst.
Picot row: K.1, *wl.fwd., k.2 tog. Rept. from * to last st., k.1.
Work 5 rows stst. Cast off loosely.
   After pressing and embroidering, fold the top over at the picot row and loosely slip-stitch the cast-off row to the inside of the bootee.

Lavender pattern

Work 4 rows stst., then pattern as follows:
1st row: K.1, wl.fwd., sl.1, k.1, p.s.s.o., k.1, *k.1, k.2 tog., wl.fwd. twice, sl.1, k.1, p.s.s.o., k.1. Rept. from * to last 4 sts., k.1, k.2 tog., wl.fwd., k.1.
2nd row: P.4, *p.2, (p.1, k.1 into long st.), p.2. Rept. from * to last 4 sts., p.4.
3rd row: K.2, wl.fwd., sl.1, k.1, p.s.s.o., *k.2 tog., wl.fwd., k.2, wl.fwd., sl.1, k.1, p.s.s.o. Rept. from * to last 4 sts., k.2 tog., wl.fwd., k.2.
4th row: P.
5th row: K.2, k.2 tog., wl.fwd., *wl.fwd., sl.1, k.1, p.s.s.o., k.2, k.2 tog., wl.fwd. Rept. from * to last 4 sts., wl.fwd., sl.1, k.1, p.s.s.o., k.2.
6th row: P.3, (p.1, k.1 into long st.), *p.4, (p.1, k.1 into long st.). Rept. from * to last 3 sts., p.3.
7th row: K.1, k.2 tog., wl.fwd., k.1, *k.1, wl.fwd., sl.1, k.1, p.s.s.o., k.2 tog., wl.fwd., k.1. Rept. from * to last 4 sts., k.1, wl.fwd., sl.1, k.1, p.s.s.o., k.1.
8th row: P.

Work 4 rows stst.

Work 2 rows moss st. (k.1, p.1) to end of 1st row, then (p.1, k.1) to end of 2nd row.

Cast off loosely in moss st.

Blue pattern

1st row: *K.2, p.2. Rept. from * to end of row.
2nd row: *P.2, k.2. Rept. from * to end of row.
3rd row: As 1st row.
4th row: As 2nd row.
Rept. these 4 rows three times.
Cast off loosely (in rib) commencing k.2.

Lemon pattern

Work 6 rows stst. then work 8 rows reversed stst. (commencing with a p. row).
Cast off loosely.

Green pattern

1st row: *K. into back of 1st st., p.1. Rept. from * to end of row.
Rept. this row 19 times.
Cast off ribwise.
(Note: Do not press ribbed section.)

The wool twist

The wool twist threaded through the illustrated examples is preferable to ribbon because it washes and dries with the garment and does not need removing and ironing each time the item is washed. It is also an "elastic" fibre and will stretch slightly if tied too firmly around the ankles or wrists.

To make a wool twist: Knot three 120 cm (60 in.) strands of wool together at each end. Anchor one end over a cupboard handle or under a chair leg. Stand back, stretching the strands taut. Place a finger inside the knot at the far end and commence turning the wool in a clockwise direction until the tightly-twisted wool starts winding back on itself when the pressure is relaxed slightly. Place a finger in the middle of the wool twist and, holding the two knotted ends together, release the anchored end. The wool will "jump" into a twist. Run it through the hand to even out the twist. This will never unravel. Thread it through a bootee or mitten, tie a knot at the end, and "tassel" the short end strands.

To make up

Press lightly on wrong side with steam iron over a cloth. Sew up the seams. Stitch the mittens straight across the finger-tip seam, or run a gathering string just above the cast-on row and draw up. Make wool twists and thread on a small safety-pin through the threading holes. Tie the bows, knot the ends of the twists, and snip 6 mm (¼ in.) below the knots. Catch the twists to the bootees or mittens at the centre under the wrists and at the back of the heels to prevent the twists becoming separated from the garment during washing.

Appendix I

Wool requirements − double-knitting

(Note that these figures are a general guide only; quantities may vary slightly with different brands of wool.)

Jumpers, cardigans and lumberjackets (with long sleeves)

		25-gram balls	50-gram balls	Oz.
46 cm	18 in.	6	3	5
51 cm	20 in.	7	4	6
56 cm	22 in.	8	4	7
61 cm	24 in.	10	5	8
66 cm	26 in.	12	6	10
71 cm	28 in.	14	7	12
76 cm	30 in.	15	8	13
81 cm	32 in.	19	10	16
86 cm	34 in.	21	11	18
91 cm	36 in.	22	11	19
96 cm	38 in.	25	13	22
101 cm	40 in.	28	14	24
106 cm	42 in.	30	15	26
111 cm	44 in.	32	16	28
116 cm	46 in.	35	18	30

1. Allow an extra 50-gram ball of wool if: (a) Using crepe wool. (b) Including a polo neck (for a polo neck in crepe wool allow 2 extra balls). (c) Making an Aran knit.
2. If making a garment with short sleeves: (a) Deduct two 50-gram balls of wool for adults' sizes. (b) Deduct one 50-gram ball for children's sizes.

Tank Tops

		25-gram balls	50-gram balls	Ozs.
56 cm	22 in.	5	3	4
61 cm	24 in.	6	3	5
66 cm	26 in.	7	4	6
71 cm	28 in.	10	5	8
76 cm	30 in.	10	5	8
81 cm	32 in.	11	6	9
86 cm	34 in.	12	6	10
91 cm	36 in.	13	7	11
96 cm	38 in.	14	7	12
102 cm	40 in.	15	8	13

All garments knitted in double-knitting wool are worked on $3\frac{1}{4}$ mm and 4 mm needles.
Tension: 11 sts. and 15 rows to 5 cm ($5\frac{1}{2}$ sts. and $7\frac{1}{2}$ rows to 1 in.).

Appendix II

Wool requirements—4-ply

(These figures provide a general guide only; quantities may vary slightly with different brands of wool.)

Jumpers, cardigans and lumberjackets (with long sleeves).

		25-gram balls	50-gram balls	Ozs.
46 cm	18 in.	5	3	4
51 cm	20 in.	6	3	5
56 cm	22 in.	7	4	6
61 cm	24 in.	8	4	7
66 cm	26 in.	10	5	8
71 cm	28 in.	11	6	9
76 cm	30 in.	13	7	11
81 cm	32 in.	14	7	12
86 cm	34 in.	16	8	14
91 cm	36 in.	18	9	15
96 cm	38 in.	19	10	16
102 cm	40 in.	21	11	18
107 cm	42 in.	23	12	20
112 cm	44 in.	25	13	22
117 cm	46 in.	28	14	24

1. Allow an extra 50-gram ball of wool if: (a) Including a polo neck. (b) Making an Aran knit.
2. If making a garment with short sleeves: (a) Deduct two 50-gram balls of wool for adults' sizes.
(b) Deduct one 50-gram ball for children's sizes.

Tank Tops

		25-gram balls	50-gram balls	Ozs.
56 cm	22 in.	4	2	3
61 cm	24 in.	5	3	4
66 cm	26 in.	6	3	5
71-86 cm	28-34 in.	7	4	6
91 cm	36 in.	8	4	7
96 cm	38 in.	10	5	8
101 cm	40 in.	11	6	9

All garments knitted in 4-ply wool are worked on $3\frac{1}{4}$ mm needles.
Tension: 7 sts. and 9 rows to 2.5 cm (1 in.).

Measurements and designs

Measurements and designs

Double Knitting

Backs (All garments except tank tops)

Size	46 / 18	51 / 20	56 / 22	61 / 24	66 / 26	71 / 28	76 / 30	81 / 32	86 / 34	91 / 36	96 / 38	102 / 40	107 / 42	112 / 44	117 / 46	cm / in.
Using size 3¼ mm needles, cast on	55	61	63	69	75	77	83	89	93	99	105	111	117	121	127	sts.
Rib for	8	8	8	8	8	10	10	10	10	12	12	14	14	14	16	rows.

Sizes 71-117 cm
Inc. 4 sts. evenly across last rib row.
Change to 4 mm needles.

	46	51	56	61	66	71	76	81	86	91	96	102	107	112	117	
Cont. straight until work measures	19	19	23	25.5	28	30.5	33	35	35	37	38	39.5	39.5	40.5	40.5	cm
	7½	7½	9	10	11	12	13	13½	14	14½	15	15½	15½	16	16	in.

or length required.

With set-in sleeves only

Armholes

	46	51	56	61	66	71	76	81	86	91	96	102	107	112	117	
Cast off at beg. next 2 rows.	2	2	2	2	3	3	3	4	4	4	4	5	5	5	5	sts.
Dec. 1 st. each end next	3	4	3	4	5	6	6	7	7	7	8	8	9	10	11	alt. rows.
	(45	49	53	57	59	63	69	71	75	81	85	89	93	95	99	sts. now rem.)
Cont. straight until armhole measures on straight	10	11.25	13	13.5	14	15	17.5	18	19.5	20.25	22	23	25.5	28	30.5	cm
	4	4½	5	5½	5½	6	6½	7	7¾	8	8½	9	10	11	12	in.

Shape shoulders

	46	51	56	61	66	71	76	81	86	91	96	102	107	112	117	
Cast off at beg. next 4 rows, then	4	5	5	5	6	6	7	7	8	8	9	9	9	9	9	sts.
at beg. foll. 2 rows.	5	4	5	6	5	7	7	8	7	9	8	8	9	9	10	sts.
Cast off remaining	19	21	23	25	25	25	27	27	29	31	33	37	39	41	43	sts.
Size	46 / 18	51 / 20	56 / 22	61 / 24	66 / 26	71 / 28	76 / 30	81 / 32	86 / 34	91 / 36	96 / 38	102 / 40	107 / 42	112 / 44	117 / 46	cm / in.

With raglan sleeves only

Armhole & raglan shapings
Cast off 2 sts. at beg. next 2 rows, then
1st row: K.2, k.2 tog., k. to last 4 sts., k.2 tog. t.b.l., k.2.

2nd row: P.
3rd row: K.
4th row: P.
Rept. these 4 rows once
then 1st and 2nd rows

only until	19	21	23	25	25	25	27	27	29	31	33	37	39	41	43	sts. rem.

Cast off.

Fronts

V-neck
As for back to armholes.

With set-in sleeves only

Armholes, dividing for v-neck

	46	51	56	61	66	71	76	81	86	91	96	102	107	112	117	
Cast off at beg. next 2 rows.			2	2	3	3	3	4	4	4	4	5	5	5	5	sts.
Next row: K.2 tog., k. turn, p. back to edge.			27	30	32	35	38	40	42	45	48	50	53	55	58	sts.
Dec. 1 st. at armhole edge for next			4	6	6	8	9	9	9	9	9	10	11	11	13	

alt. rows, at the same
time dec. 1 st. at neck
edge in next and foll.

4th rows until			15	16	17	19	21	22	23	25	26	26	27	27	28	sts. rem.

Cont. straight until the
armhole matches the
back armhole.

Shape shoulder

Cast off at shoulder edge of next 2 alt. rows and			5	5	6	6	7	7	8	8	9	9	9	9	9	sts.
then rem.			5	6	5	7	7	8	7	8	9	8	9	9	10	sts.

Join in wool at v., slip
next st. onto a
safety-pin.

With raglan sleeves only

Armholes, raglan shapings, dividing for v-neck
Cast off 2 sts. at beg. of
next 2 rows, then
1st row: K.2, k.2 tog., k.
until 4 sts. remain,
k.2 tog. t.b.l., k.2.
2nd row: P.
3rd row: K.
4th row: P.

Size	46 / 18	51 / 20	56 / 22	61 / 24	66 / 26	71 / 28	76 / 30	81 / 32	86 / 34	91 / 36	96 / 38	102 / 40	107 / 42	112 / 44	117 / 46	cm / in.
Next row: K.2, k.2 tog., k. turn, leaving sts. for the other side until required.			28	31	33	36	39	41	43	46	49	51	54	55	58	sts.

Next row: P. back to edge.
Next row: K.
Next row: P.
Cont. raglan shapings by repeating 1st and 2nd rows above only and at the same time dec. 1 st. at the neck edge in the next and foll. 4th rows until decreasings have been completed at the neck edge.

	46 / 18	51 / 20	56 / 22	61 / 24	66 / 26	71 / 28	76 / 30	81 / 32	86 / 34	91 / 36	96 / 38	102 / 40	107 / 42	112 / 44	117 / 46	
			9	10	11	12	12	13	13	15	17	18	19	20	22	

Cont. raglan shapings only until 2 sts. remain. K.2 tog. Fasten off. Join in wool at v, slip next st. onto a safety-pin and leave aside. Work 2nd side to match, reversing the shapings and noting that all k.2 togs. will be t.b.l.

Crew, turtle & polo necks

With set-in sleeves only

	46 / 18	51 / 20	56 / 22	61 / 24	66 / 26	71 / 28	76 / 30	81 / 32	86 / 34	91 / 36	96 / 38	102 / 40	107 / 42	112 / 44	117 / 46	
As for back until	45	50	53	57	59	63	69	71	75	81	85	89	93	95	99	sts. rem.
Continue straight until armhole measures (on straight)	5 / 2	5.75 / 2¼	6 / 2½	6 / 2½	7 / 2¾	7.5 / 3	8 / 3¼	9 / 3½	9 / 3½	9.5 / 3¾	10 / 4	11.5 / 4½	12.5 / 5	15 / 6		cm / in

less than back armhole when measured straight down from highest point.
Shape neck.

	46 / 18	51 / 20	56 / 22	61 / 24	66 / 26	71 / 28	76 / 30	81 / 32	86 / 34	91 / 36	96 / 38	102 / 40	107 / 42	112 / 44	117 / 46	
K.	17	19	21	23	24	26	29	30	31	34	35	37	38	39	41	sts.
Cast off next	11	11	11	11	11	11	11	11	13	13	15	15	17	17	17	sts.

K. to end. Working on the last set of sts.:
Next row: P. to last 2 sts., p.2 tog.
Next row: K.

Size	46	51	56	61	66	71	76	81	86	91	96	102	107	112	117	cm
	18	20	22	24	26	28	30	32	34	36	38	40	42	44	46	ins
Rept. last 2 rows	3	4	3	4	5	6	7	7	7	8	8	10	10	11	12	times.

Cont. straight until armhole matches back armhole.

Shape shoulders

	46	51	56	61	66	71	76	81	86	91	96	102	107	112	117	
Cast off	4	5	4	5	5	6	7	7	8	8	9	9	9	9	9	sts.
at beg. next 2 alt. rows, then	5	4	5	4	5	7	7	8	7	9	8	8	9	9	10	sts.

at beg. foll. alt. row. Cast off.

Join in wool at neck edge and complete the other side to match, reversing the shapings.

With raglan sleeves only

	46	51	56	61	66	71	76	81	86	91	96	102	107	112	117	
As for back until	39	41	43	45	47	49	51	51	53	55	57	61	63	65	67	sts. rem.

Next row: K.2, k.2 tog.

	46	51	56	61	66	71	76	81	86	91	96	102	107	112	117	
k.	11	11	12	12	14	15	14	14	15	16	17	19	19	20	22	sts.
Cast off next	11	11	11	11	11	11	13	13	15	15	15	15	17	17	17	sts.

Work to last 4 sts., k.2 tog. t.b.l., k.2. Working on the last set of sts. and continuing the raglan shapings as before, dec. 1 st. at neck edge on every alt. row

	46	51	56	61	66	71	76	81	86	91	96	102	107	112	117	
	5	5	5	7	7	8	8	8	8	7	8	9	9	10	10	times.

Cont. raglan shapings only until 2 sts. remain. K.2 tog., fasten off.

Join in wool at neck edge and complete the other side to match, reversing the shapings.

High-necked cardigan

(See notes on buttonholes before commencing.)

Size	46 / 18	51 / 20	56 / 22	61 / 24	66 / 26	71 / 28	76 / 30	81 / 32	86 / 34	91 / 36	96 / 38	102 / 40	107 / 42	112 / 44	117 / 46	cm / ins

Left front
Using 3¼ mm needles, cast on **31 34 35 38 41 44 47 49 51 55 57 60 63 65 69** sts.
(This includes 6 sts. for the front ribbed border.)
Rib for **8 8 8 8 8 10 10 10 10 12 12 14 14 14 16** rows.
Change to 4 mm needles and, keeping the 6 border sts. in rib, cont. straight until the front matches the back length to armhole.

With set-in sleeves only
Armhole
Cast off **2 2 2 2 3 3 3 4 4 4 4 5 5 6 6** sts. at armhole edge, then dec. 1 st. at armhole edge on foll. **3 4 3 4 5 6 6 7 7 7 8 8 9 10 11** alt. rows

Cont. straight until armhole measures (on straight)
cm: **5 5.75 6 6 7 7.5 8 9 9 9.5 10 11.5 11.5 12.5 15**
in.: **2 2¼ 2½ 2½ 2¾ 3 3¼ 3½ 3½ 3¾ 4 4½ 4½ 5 6**
less than back armhole, when measured straight down from the highest point.

At neck edge
If adding a round neckband: rib 6 and cast off next **5 5 5 5 5 5 6 5 6 7 7 7 8 8 9** sts.

(Place the first 6 sts. on a safety-pin on completion of the work.)
If adding a collar: cast off the first 6 sts.
Cast off next **5 5 5 5 5 5 6 5 6 7 7 7 8 8 9** sts.

All styles
Dec. 1 st. at neck edge on foll. **2 3 2 4 5 5 5 4 4 6 6 7 8 8 8** alt. rows.

Cont. straight until armhole measures the same as the back armhole.

Size	46	51	56	61	66	71	76	81	86	91	96	102	107	112	117	cm
	18	20	22	24	26	28	30	32	34	36	38	40	42	44	46	ins

Shape shoulder
Cast off

4	5	5	5	6	6	7	7	8	8	9	9	9	9	9	sts.

at shoulder edge of next
2 rows, then cast off the
remaining shoulder sts.
Place the 6 remaining
border sts. onto a
safety-pin, if adding a
neckband.
Right front
As for left front,
reversing the shapings.

With raglan sleeves only
Left front
Armholes & raglan
shapings
Cast off 2 sts. at
armhole edge, k. to last
6 sts., rib 6.
Next row: Rib 6, p. to end.
1st row: K.2, k.2 tog., k.
to last 6 sts., rib 6.
2nd row: Rib 6, p. to
end.
3rd row: K. to last 6 sts.,
rib 6.
4th row: Rib 6, p. to
end.
Rept. these 4 rows
once, then 1st and 2nd
rows only until armhole
measures (on straight)

5	5.7	6	6	7	7.5	8	9	9	9.5	10	11.5	11.5	12.5	15	cm
2	2¼	2½	2½	2¾	3	3¼	3½	3½	3¾	4	4½	4½	5	5½	in.

less than the back
armhole, when
measured straight down
from the highest point.
Neck
If adding a round
neckband: rib 6 and
cast off next

5	5	5	5	5	5	6	5	6	7	7	7	8	8	9	sts.

(Place the first 6 sts. on
a safety-pin on
completion of the
front.)
If adding a collar: cast
off these 6 sts.
Cast off next

5	5	5	5	5	5	6	5	6	7	7	7	8	8	9	sts.

All styles
Cont. raglan shapings

Size	46	51	56	61	66	71	76	81	86	91	96	102	107	112	117	cm
	18	20	22	24	26	28	30	32	34	36	38	40	42	44	46	ins

and dec. 1 st. at neck
edge on foll.

	46	51	56	61	66	71	76	81	86	91	96	102	107	112	117	
	2	3	2	4	5	5	5	4	4	6	6	7	8	8	8	alt. rows.

Cont. raglan shapings
only until 2 sts. remain.
K.2 tog. Fasten off.
Right front
As for left front,
reversing the shapings
and noting that the
k.2 togs. will be t.b.l.

V-necked cardigan
(See notes on buttonholes before commencing.)
Left front
As for high-necked
cardigan to armhole.
Discontinue
buttonholes near this
point.

With set-in sleeves only

Armhole
Cast off

	46	51	56	61	66	71	76	81	86	91	96	102	107	112	117	
	2	2	2	2	3	3	3	4	4	4	4	5	5	5	5	sts.

at armhole edge. K. to
last 8 sts., k.2 tog., rib 6.
Next row: Rib 6, p. to
end.
Dec. 1 st. at armhole
edge for next

	46	51	56	61	66	71	76	81	86	91	96	102	107	112	117	
	3	4	4	6	6	8	9	8	9	9	9	10	12	13	14	alt. rows.

At the same time dec.
1 st. at inside front
border on every 4th
row until

	46	51	56	61	66	71	76	81	86	91	96	102	107	112	117	
	19	20	21	22	23	25	27	29	30	31	32	33	33	34	35	sts. rem.

Cont. straight until
armhole matches back
armhole.
Shape shoulder
Cast off

	46	51	56	61	66	71	76	81	86	91	96	102	107	112	117	
	4	5	5	5	6	6	7	7	8	8	9	9	9	9	9	sts.

at shoulder edge of next
2 alt. rows, then
remaining

	46	51	56	61	66	71	76	81	86	91	96	102	107	112	117	
	5	4	5	6	5	7	7	8	7	9	8	8	9	9	10	sts.

Cont. on 6 border sts.
only until sufficiently
long to reach half-way
across back neck. Cast
off.

Size	46	51	56	61	66	71	76	81	86	91	96	102	107	112	117	cm
	18	20	22	24	26	28	30	32	34	36	38	40	42	44	46	ins

Right front
As for left front,
reversing the shapings.

With raglan sleeves only
*Armhole & raglan
shapings*
Cast off 2 sts. at
armhole edge, k. to last
6 sts., rib 6.
Next row: Rib 6, p. to
end.
1st row: K.2, k.2 tog., k.
to last 8 sts., k.2 tog.,
rib 6.
2nd row: Rib 6, p. to
end.
3rd row: K. to last 6 sts.,
rib 6.
4th row: Rib 6, p. to
end.
Rept. these 4 rows
once. Dec. 1 st. inside
front border every 4th

	46	51	56	61	66	71	76	81	86	91	96	102	107	112	117	
row until	6	8	9	10	11	12	12	13	13	15	17	18	19	20	22	

decreasings have been
completed. At the same
time continuing the
raglan shapings as
follows:
Next row: K.2, k.2 tog.,
k. to last 6 sts., rib 6.
Next row: Rib 6, p. to
end.
Rept. these 2 rows until
only the 6 border sts.
remain. Cont. on these
6 sts. until work is of
sufficient length to
reach half-way across
the back neck. Cast off.
Right front
As for left front,
reversing the shapings
and noting that the
k.2 togs. will be t.b.l.

Lumberjacket

Using 3¼ mm needles,	46	51	56	61	66	71	76	81	86	91	96	102	107	112	117	
cast on			31	34	37	40	43	46	49	52	55	58	61	64	67	sts.
Rib for			8	8	8	10	10	10	10	12	12	14	14	14	16	rows.

Size	46 / 18	51 / 20	56 / 22	61 / 24	66 / 26	71 / 28	76 / 30	81 / 32	86 / 34	91 / 36	96 / 38	102 / 40	107 / 42	112 / 44	117 / 46	cm / ins

Change to 4 mm needles. Cont. straight until work measures same as back to armhole.

With set-in sleeves only

Left front
Armholes
Cast off at armhole edge, then dec. 1 st. at armhole edge on foll.

	46	51	56	61	66	71	76	81	86	91	96	102	107	112	117	
Cast off			2	2	3	3	3	4	4	4	4	5	5	6	6	sts.
dec. 1 st. foll.			3	4	5	6	6	7	7	7	8	8	9	9	11	alt. rows.

Cont. straight until armhole measures on straight

	46	51	56	61	66	71	76	81	86	91	96	102	107	112	117	
			6.5	6.5	7	7.5	8	9	9	9.5	10	11.5	11.5	12.5	15	cm
			2½	2½	2¾	3	3¼	3½	3½	3¾	4	4½	4½	5	6	in.

less than back armhole when measured down from the highest point on the shoulder.
At neck edge cast off and dec. 1 st. at neck edge on foll.

	46	51	56	61	66	71	76	81	86	91	96	102	107	112	117	
cast off			8	8	8	8	8	8	8	8	9	10	10	11	11	sts.
dec. 1 st. foll.			3	4	4	4	5	5	7	8	8	9	10	11	11	alt. rows.

Cont. straight until armhole measures same as back armhole.
Shape shoulder
Cast off at shoulder edge of next 2 alt. rows, and then remaining

	46	51	56	61	66	71	76	81	86	91	96	102	107	112	117	
Cast off			5	5	6	6	7	7	8	8	9	9	9	9	9	sts.
remaining			5	6	5	7	7	8	7	9	8	8	9	9	10	sts.

Right front
As for left front, reversing the shapings.

With raglan sleeves only

Left front
Armholes & raglan shapings
Cast off 2 sts. at armhole edge, k. to end.
Next row: P.
1st row: K.2, k.2 tog., k. to end.
2nd row: P.
3rd row: K.

63

Size	46 / 18	51 / 20	56 / 22	61 / 24	66 / 26	71 / 28	76 / 30	81 / 32	86 / 34	91 / 36	96 / 38	102 / 40	107 / 42	112 / 44	117 / 46	cm / ins

4th row: P.
Rept. these 4 rows
once, then 1st and 2nd
rows only until armhole
measures
less than back armhole,
when measured down
from the highest point
on the shoulder.

	46	51	56	61	66	71	76	81	86	91	96	102	107	112	117	
measures			6.5	6.5	7	7.5	8	9	9	9.5	10	11.5	11.5	12.5	15	cm
			2½	2½	2¾	3	3¼	3½	3½	3¾	4	4½	4½	5	6	in.

At neck edge, cast off
and, continuing raglan
shapings, dec. 1 st. at

	56	61	66	71	76	81	86	91	96	102	107	112	117	
neck edge on foll.	8	8	8	8	8	8	8	8	9	10	10	11	11	sts.

At neck edge, cast off and, continuing raglan shapings, dec. 1 st. at neck edge on foll.

	56	61	66	71	76	81	86	91	96	102	107	112	117	
	3	4	4	4	5	5	7	8	8	9	10	11	11	alt. rows.

Cont. raglan shapings
until only 2 sts. remain.
K.2 tog. Fasten off.
Right front
As for left front,
reversing the shapings
and noting that the
k.2 togs. will be t.b.l.

Sleeves

Long sleeves

(Both alike)
Using 3¼ mm needles,

	46	51	56	61	66	71	76	81	86	91	96	102	107	112	117	
cast on	33	33	33	35	37	39	41	43	45	49	53	53	57	61	63	sts.
Rib for	8	8	8	8	8	10	10	10	10	12	12	14	14	14	16	rows.

Change to 4 mm
needles and work
4 rows.
Inc. 1 st. at each end of
next and every foll. 8th

	46	51	56	61	66	71	76	81	86	91	96	102	107	112	117	
row until	45	45	47	51	55	59	63	67	71	75	79	83	87	91	93	sts. rem.

Cont. straight until

	46	51	56	61	66	71	76	81	86	91	96	102	107	112	117	
sleeve edge measures	20	21.5	23	25.5	28	33	35.5	38	40.5	43	46	48.25	48.25	48.25	48.25	cm
	8	8½	9	10	11	13	14	15	16	17	18	19	19	19	19	in.

With set-in sleeve tops only

	46	51	56	61	66	71	76	81	86	91	96	102	107	112	117	
Cast off	2	2	2	2	3	3	3	4	4	4	4	5	5	5	5	sts

at beg. next 2 rows,
then dec. 1 st. at each
end of next 6 rows.
Work 1 row without
shaping.

Size	46	51		56	61	66	71	76	81	86	91		96	102	107	112	117	cm
	18	20		22	24	26	28	30	32	34	36		38	40	42	44	46	in.

1st row: Dec. 1 st. at each end.
2nd row: Dec. 1 st. at each end.
3rd row: Work without shaping.

| Rept. last 3 rows until | 17 | 19 | | 21 | 21 | 25 | 27 | 27 | 29 | 29 | 29 | | 31 | 31 | 31 | 33 | 33 | sts. rem. |

Dec. 1 st. at each end of

| next | 3 | 4 | | 4 | 4 | 5 | 6 | 6 | 7 | 7 | 7 | | 7 | 7 | 7 | 8 | 8 | rows. |

Cast off.

With raglan sleeve tops only

Cast off 2 sts. at beg. next 2 rows.
1st row: K.2, k.2 tog., k. to last 4 sts., k.2 tog. t.b.l., k.2.
2nd row: P.
3rd row: K.
4th row: P.
Rept. these 4 rows once.
Then rept. 1st and 2nd rows only until 7 sts. remain. Cast off.

Short sleeves

(Both alike)
Using 3¾ mm needles,

| cast on | 41 | 41 | | 41 | 45 | 47 | 51 | 55 | 57 | 61 | 65 | | 67 | 71 | 73 | 87 | 89 | sts. |
| Rib for | 8 | 8 | | 8 | 8 | 8 | 10 | 10 | 10 | 12 | 12 | | 14 | 14 | 14 | 14 | 16 | rows. |

Change to 4 mm needles.
Inc. 1 st. at each end of next and every foll. 4th

| row until there are | 45 | 45 | | 47 | 51 | 55 | 59 | 63 | 67 | 71 | 75 | | 79 | 83 | 87 | 91 | 93 | sts. |

Cont. straight until

| sleeve edge measures | 6.5 | 6.5 | | 6.5 | 6.5 | 6.5 | 7 | 7.5 | 7.5 | 9 | 9 | | 10 | 13 | 13.5 | 14 | 15.25 | cm |
| | 2½ | 2½ | | 2½ | 2½ | 2½ | 2¾ | 3 | 3 | 3½ | 3½ | | 4 | 5 | 5¼ | 5½ | 6 | ins. |

With set-in sleeve tops only

As for set-in sleeve tops of long sleeve instructions.

With raglan sleeve tops only

As for raglan sleeve tops of long sleeve instructions.

Neckbands, collars and armbands

Crew, turtle & polo neckbands

Size	46 / 18	51 / 20	56 / 22	61 / 24	66 / 26	71 / 28	76 / 30	81 / 32	86 / 34	91 / 36	96 / 38	102 / 40	107 / 42	112 / 44	117 / 46	cm / in.

With set-in sleeves only

Join one shoulder seam. Open out.

With raglan sleeves only

Stitch sleeves to front and back, leaving one seam open. Open out.
All sizes
Using 3¼ mm needles, pick up and k. evenly around neck.

Size	46/18	51/20	56/22	61/24	66/26	71/28	76/30	81/32	86/34	91/36	96/38	102/40	107/42	112/44	117/46	
pick up and k.	60	68	74	82	86	92	96	100	104	108	112	116	120	124	128	sts.

Crew neck only

Work 8 rows for a single neckband. Cast off.
Work 16 rows for a double neckband. Cast off. Fold the band to the inside and catch loosely all round.

Turtle neck only
Work 26 rows. Cast off. Fold to the inside and catch loosely all round.

Polo neck only
Work 10 cm (4 in.) for a child's size, 15 cm (6 in.) for a lady's and 18 cm (7 in.) for a man's size. Fold in half to the outside.

Round neck bands (for high-necked cardigans)

Using 3¼ mm needles, pick up and k. evenly around the neck. This figure includes the border sts. from the two safety-pins.

	66	70	75	79	85	95	101	105	109	117	121	125	129	133	135	sts.

Size	46 / 18	51 / 20	56 / 22	61 / 24	66 / 26	71 / 28	76 / 30	81 / 32	86 / 34	91 / 36	96 / 38	102 / 40	107 / 42	112 / 44	117 / 46	cm in.

Work 8 rows in rib, making a buttonhole over the 4th and 5th rows of the neckband.

Collars (for lumberjackets and high-necked cardigans)

Using 3¼ mm needles, cast on

46	51	56	61	66	71	76	81	86	91	96	102	107	112	117	
55	59	67	73	77	81	85	89	93	97	101	105	109	113	115	sts.

Rib for 22 rows for a child's garment, 24 rows for a lady's garment and 26 rows for a man's garment.
Cast off.

V-neckband

With set-in sleeves only

Join right shoulder seam.

With raglan sleeves only

Stitch sleeve raglan shapings to front and back raglan shapings leaving one seam open. Open out.

All styles

Using 3¼ mm needles and with r.s.f., pick up and k.

46	51	56	61	66	71	76	81	86	91	96	102	107	112	117	
		89	94	106	109	119	123	133	139	143	149	153	159	163	sts.

including the st. from the safety-pin. Mark this st. with a coloured thread.
1st row: Rib until 2 sts. before the centre (marked) st., k.2 tog. t.b.l., p.1, k.2 tog., rib to end.
2nd row: Rib until 2 sts. before the centre (marked) st., p.2 tog., k.1, p.2 tog. t.b.l., rib to end.
Rept. these 2 rows 3 times. Cast off.

Armbands (for sleeveless v-necked pullover)

Size	46	51	56	61	66	71	76	81	86	91	96	102	107	112	117	cm
	18	20	22	24	26	28	30	32	34	36	38	40	42	44	46	in.
Stitch left shoulder seam and neckband. Using 3¼ mm needles and with r.s.f., pick up and k. evenly around the armhole. Rib for 8 rows. Cast off.			82	88	94	100	106	116	120	122	126	130	136	142	148	sts.

Tank tops

Back

Size	61	66	71	76	81	86	91	96	102	cm
	24	26	28	30	32	34	36	38	40	ins
Using 3¼ mm needles, cast on	69	73	79	83	87	93	99	105	111	sts.
Work in rib for 8 cm (3¼ in.) for a child's garment, 10 cm (4 in.) for a lady's garment and 12 cm (4¾ in.) for a man's garment. Change to 4 mm needles. Cont. in stst. until work measures	16.5	16.5	18	20	23	25.5	25.5	28	30.5	cm.
	6½	6½	7	8	9	10	10	11	12	in.
Armholes Cast off 6 sts. at beg. next 2 rows. Dec. 1 st. at each end of every alt. row until	45	49	53	57	63	67	71	75	79	sts. rem.
Work straight until armhole measures (on straight)	12.5	13.75	15	16.25	20	21	22	24	25	cm.
	5	5½	6	6½	8	8¼	8¾	9½	10	in.
Shape shoulders Cast off	4	5	5	6	6	6	7	7	8	sts.
at beg. of next 4 rows, then	5	5	6	5	6	7	7	8	8	sts.
at beg. of next 2 alt. rows. Cast off remaining	19	19	21	23	27	29	29	31	31	sts.

Front

Size	61	66	71	76	81	86	91	96	102	cm
	24	26	28	30	32	34	36	38	40	in.

As for back until
armhole decreasings
have been completed

and	45	49	53	57	63	67	71	75	79	sts. rem.

Shape neck

K.	15	16	17	19	21	23	24	26	27	sts.
Cast off next	15	17	19	19	21	21	23	23	25	sts.

K. to end. Dec. 1 st. at
neck edge on next alt.

rows until	13	15	16	17	18	19	21	22	24	sts. rem.

Work straight until
armhole matches back
armhole, finishing at the
shoulder edge.

Shape shoulder

Cast off	4	5	5	6	6	6	7	7	8	sts.
at beg. next 2 alt. rows, then	5	5	6	5	6	7	7	8	8	sts.

at shoulder edge in next
alt. row.
Join in wool at neck
edge and work to
match completed side,
reversing the shapings.

Neck and armhole bands

Neckbands
Stitch right shoulder
seam. Using 3¼ mm
needles and with r.s.f.,

pick up and k.	102	112	122	134	144	156	160	168	178	sts.

evenly around the neck.
Rib for 6 rows. Cast Off.

Armbands
Stitch left shoulder
seam and neckband.
Using 3¼ mm needles

and r.s.f., pick up and k.	89	94	100	106	116	120	124	132	136	sts.

evenly around the
armhole. Rib for 6 rows.
Cast off.

4-ply

Backs (All garments except tank tops)

Size	46 / 18	51 / 20	56 / 22	61 / 24	66 / 26	71 / 28	76 / 30	81 / 32	86 / 34	91 / 36	96 / 38	102 / 40	107 / 42	112 / 44	117 / 46	cm / ins
Using 2¾ mm needles, cast on	71	79	85	91	99	101	109	117	125	131	139	147	155	163	171	sts.
Rib for	8	8	8	8	10	10	12	12	14	14	16	16	18	18	18	rows.

Sizes 71-117 cm only
Inc. 6 sts. evenly across last rib row.
Change to 3¼ mm needles.

All sizes

	46 / 18	51 / 20	56 / 22	61 / 24	66 / 26	71 / 28	76 / 30	81 / 32	86 / 34	91 / 36	96 / 38	102 / 40	107 / 42	112 / 44	117 / 46	
Cont. straight until work measures	19	19	23	25.5	28	30.5	33	35	35	37	38	39.5	39.5	40.5	40.5	cm.
	7½	7½	9	10	11	12	13	13½	14	14½	15	15½	15½	16	16	in.

or length required.

With set-in sleeves only

Armholes

	46 / 18	51 / 20	56 / 22	61 / 24	66 / 26	71 / 28	76 / 30	81 / 32	86 / 34	91 / 36	96 / 38	102 / 40	107 / 42	112 / 44	117 / 46	
Cast off at beg. next 2 rows.	3	3	3	4	4	5	5	6	6	7	7	8	8	9	9	sts.
Dec. 1 st. each end next and every foll. alt. row until	63	65	67	71	77	83	89	95	101	109	113	115	119	123	125	sts. rem.
Cont. straight until armhole measures (on straight)	10	11.25	13	14	14	15	17.5	18	19.5	20.25	22	23	25.5	28	30.5	cm.
	4	4½	5	5½	5½	6	6½	7	7¾	8	8½	9	10	11	12	in.

Shape shoulders

	46 / 18	51 / 20	56 / 22	61 / 24	66 / 26	71 / 28	76 / 30	81 / 32	86 / 34	91 / 36	96 / 38	102 / 40	107 / 42	112 / 44	117 / 46	
Cast off at beg. next 4 rows, then	7	7	7	7	8	9	9	10	11	12	12	12	13	13	13	sts.
at beg. foll. 2 rows. Cast	7	7	7	8	8	8	10	10	10	11	12	13	12	13	14	sts.
off remaining	21	23	25	27	29	31	33	35	37	39	41	41	43	45	45	sts.

With raglan sleeves only

Armhole & raglan shapings

	46 / 18	51 / 20	56 / 22	61 / 24	66 / 26	71 / 28	76 / 30	81 / 32	86 / 34	91 / 36	96 / 38	102 / 40	107 / 42	112 / 44	117 / 46	
Cast off at beg. next 2 rows, then:	2	2	2	3	4	5	6	7	8	9	10	10	10	10	10	sts.

1st row: K.3, k.2 tog., k. to last 5 sts., k.2 tog. t.b.l., k.3.
2nd row: P.

	46 / 18	51 / 20	56 / 22	61 / 24	66 / 26	71 / 28	76 / 30	81 / 32	86 / 34	91 / 36	96 / 38	102 / 40	107 / 42	112 / 44	117 / 46	cm / ins

3rd row: K.
4th row: P.
Rept. these 4 rows twice, then 1st and 2nd rows only until remain.

| | 21 | 23 | 25 | 27 | 29 | 31 | 33 | 35 | 37 | 39 | 41 | 41 | 43 | 45 | 45 | sts. |

Cast off.

Fronts

V-necked jerseys

As for back to armholes.

With set-in sleeves only

Armholes, dividing for v-neck
Cast off

| | | | 3 | 4 | 4 | 5 | 5 | 6 | 6 | 7 | 7 | 8 | 8 | 9 | 9 | sts. |

at beg. next 2 rows.
Next row: K.2 tog., k.

| | | | 37 | 39 | 43 | 46 | 50 | 50 | 57 | 59 | 62 | 66 | 70 | 73 | 77 | sts., |

turn, p. back to edge.
Dec. 1 st. at armhole edge for next

| | | | 6 | 6 | 7 | 7 | 8 | 8 | 9 | 7 | 8 | 11 | 13 | 14 | 17 | alt. rows. |

At the same time dec. 1 st. at neck edge in next and foll. 4th rows until

| | | | 21 | 22 | 24 | 26 | 28 | 30 | 32 | 35 | 36 | 37 | 38 | 39 | 40 | sts. rem. |

Cont. straight until armhole matches back armhole.
Shape shoulders
Cast off

| | | | 7 | 7 | 8 | 9 | 9 | 10 | 11 | 12 | 12 | 12 | 13 | 13 | 13 | sts. |

at shoulder edge of next 2 alt. rows, and then rem.

| | | | 7 | 8 | 8 | 8 | 10 | 10 | 10 | 11 | 12 | 13 | 12 | 13 | 14 | sts. |

Join in wool at v, slip next st. onto a safety-pin and leave aside. Work 2nd side to match, reversing the shapings.

With raglan sleeves only

Armholes, raglan shapings, dividing for v-neck
Cast off

| | | | 2 | 3 | 4 | 5 | 6 | 7 | 8 | 9 | 10 | 10 | 10 | 10 | 10 | sts. |

at beg. of next 2 rows, then:
1st row: K.3, k.2 tog., k. until 5 sts. remain, k.2 tog. t.b.l., k.3.
2nd row: P.
3rd row: K.

Size	46	51	56	61	66	71	76	81	86	91	96	102	107	112	117	cm
	18	20	22	24	26	28	30	32	34	36	38	40	42	44	46	ins

4th row: P.
Next row: K.3, k.2 tog.,
k.

| | | | 35 | 37 | 40 | 43 | 43 | 49 | 52 | 54 | 56 | 61 | 65 | 69 | 73 | sts., |

turn, leaving sts. for
other side until required.
Next row P. back to edge.
Next row: K.
Next row: P.
Cont. raglan shapings
by repeating 1st and
2nd rows above only
and, at the same time,
dec. 1 st. at neck edge
in next and foll. 4th
rows until

| | | | 8 | 10 | 11 | 12 | 13 | 14 | 14 | 15 | 16 | 17 | 18 | 19 | 19 | sts. rem. |

Cont. raglan shapings
only until 2 sts. remain.
K.2 tog. Fasten off.
Join in wool at v, slip
next st. onto a
safety-pin and leave
aside. Work 2nd side to
match, reversing the
shapings and noting all
k.2 togs. will be t.b.l.

Crew, turtle & polo necked jerseys
With set-in sleeves only

As for back until

| | 63 | 65 | 67 | 71 | 77 | 83 | 89 | 95 | 101 | 109 | 113 | 115 | 119 | 123 | 125 | sts. rem. |

Continue straight until
armhole measures (on
straight)

| | 5 | 5.75 | 6 | 6 | 7 | 7.5 | 8 | 9 | 9 | 9.5 | 10 | 11.5 | 12.5 | 15 | | c-m |
| | 2 | 2¼ | 2½ | 2½ | 2¾ | 3 | 3¼ | 3½ | 3½ | 3¾ | 4 | 4½ | 5 | 6 | | in. |

less than back armhole
when measured straight
down from highest
point.
Shape neck
K.

| | 27 | 28 | 28 | 30 | 32 | 35 | 37 | 40 | 41 | 45 | 46 | 47 | 48 | 50 | 50 | sts. |

Cast off next

| | 9 | 9 | 11 | 11 | 13 | 13 | 15 | 15 | 19 | 19 | 21 | 21 | 23 | 23 | 25 | sts. |

k. to end. Working on
last set of sts.:
Next row: P. to last
2 sts., p.2 tog.
Next row: K.
Rept. last 2 rows until

| | 21 | 21 | 21 | 22 | 24 | 26 | 28 | 30 | 32 | 35 | 36 | 37 | 38 | 39 | 40 | sts. rem. |

Cont. straight until
armhole matches back
armhole.

Size	46	51	56	61	66	71	76	81	86	91	96	102	107	112	117	cm
	18	20	22	24	26	28	30	32	34	36	38	40	42	44	46	ins

Shape shoulders
Cast off
at beg. next 2 alt. rows,

7	7	7	7	8	9	9	10	11	12	12	12	13	13	13	sts.

then
at beg. foll. alt. row.
Join in wool at neck
edge and complete the
other side to match,
reversing the shapings.

7	7	7	8	8	8	10	10	10	11	12	13	12	13	14	sts.

With raglan sleeves only

As for back until

49	51	53	57	61	63	65	67	69	73	77	79	83	85	87	sts. rem.

Next row: K.3, k.2 tog.,
k.

15	16	16	18	19	20	20	21	20	22	23	24	25	26	26	sts.

Cast off next

9	9	11	11	13	13	15	15	19	19	21	21	23	23	25	sts.

Work to last 5 sts.,
k. tog. t.b.l., k.3.
Working on last set of
sts. and continuing
raglan shapings as
before, dec. 1 st. at
neck edge until

9	9	10	10	10	12	12	12	13	13	14	13	14	13	14	sts. rem.

Cont. raglan shapings
only until 2 sts. remain.
K.2 tog. Fasten off.
Join in wool at neck
edge and complete the
other side of the front
to match, reversing the
shapings and noting
that k.2 togs. will be
t.b.l.

High-necked cardigan

(See notes on buttonholes before commencing.)
Left front
Using 2¾ mm needles,
cast on
(This includes 9 sts. for
the front ribbed
border.)

40	44	46	50	54	58	62	66	70	74	78	82	86	90	94	sts.

Rib for
Change to 3¼ mm
needles and, keeping
the 9 border sts. in rib,
continue straight until

8	8	8	8	10	10	12	12	14	14	16	16	18	18	18	rows.

the work measures

19	19	23	25.5	28	30.5	33	35	35	37	38	39.5	39.5	40.5	40.5	cm.
7½	7½	9	10	11	12	13	13½	14	14½	15	15½	15½	16	16	in.

Size	46 18	51 20	56 22	61 24	66 26	71 28	76 30	81 32	86 34	91 36	96 38	102 40	107 42	112 44	117 46	cm in.

With set-in sleeves only

Armhole

Cast off at armhole edge, then dec. 1 st. at armhole edge on foll.

	46 18	51 20	56 22	61 24	66 26	71 28	76 30	81 32	86 34	91 36	96 38	102 40	107 42	112 44	117 46	
	3	3	3	4	4	5	5	6	6	7	7	8	8	9	9	sts.
	4	6	6	6	7	7	8	8	9	7	8	11	13	14	17	alt. rows.

Cont. straight until armhole measures (on straight)

	5	5.75	6.5	6.5	7	8	8	9	9	9.5	10	11.5	11.5	12.5	15	cm
	2	2¼	2½	2½	2¾	3¼	3¼	3½	3½	3¾	4	4½	4½	5	6	in.

less than back armhole, measuring down from highest shoulder point.

At neck edge

If adding a round neckband, rib 9 and place these sts. on safety-pin on completion of the front. Cast off these 9 border sts. if adding a collar.

Cast off next

	2	3	3	3	4	4	4	4	5	6	7	7	7	8	7	sts.

Dec. 1 st. at neck edge on next

	1	2	4	5	5	7	6	8	8	9	9	10	10	11	12	alt. rows.

Cont. straight until armhole measures same as back armhole.

Shape shoulder

Cast off at shoulder edge of next 2 alt. rows, and then

	7	7	7	7	8	9	9	10	11	12	12	12	13	13	13	sts.

remaining

	7	7	7	8	8	8	10	10	10	11	12	13	12	13	14	sts.

Right front

As for left front, reversing the shapings.

With raglan sleeves only

Armholes and raglan shapings

Cast off at armhole edge, k. to last 9 sts., rib 9.

	2	2	2	3	4	5	6	7	8	9	10	10	10	10	10	sts.

Next row: Rib 9, p. to end.
1st row: K.3, k.2 tog., k. to last 9 sts., rib 9.
2nd row: Rib 9, p. to end.
3rd row: K. to last 9 sts., rib 9.
4th row: Rib 9, p. to end.

Size	46 / 18	51 / 20	56 / 22	61 / 24	66 / 26	71 / 28	76 / 30	81 / 32	86 / 34	91 / 36	96 / 38	102 / 40	107 / 42	112 / 44	117 / 46	cm / in.

Rept. these 4 rows twice, then 1st and 2nd rows only until armhole measures

	46	51	56	61	66	71	76	81	86	91	96	102	107	112	117	cm/in
	5	5.75	6	6	7	7.5	8	9	9	9.5	10	11.5	11.5	12.5	15	cm
	2	2¼	2½	2½	2¾	3	3¼	3½	3½	3¾	4	4½	4½	5	5½	in.

less than back armhole, when measuring down from the highest shoulder point.

At neck edge
If adding round neckband, rib 9 and place these sts. on safety-pin on completion of the front. Cast off these 9 border sts. if adding a collar. Cast off next

| | 2 | 3 | 3 | 3 | 4 | 4 | 4 | 4 | 5 | 6 | 7 | 7 | 7 | 7 | 8 | sts. |

Cont. raglan shapings, and dec. 1 st. at neck edge on foll.

| | 1 | 2 | 4 | 5 | 5 | 7 | 6 | 8 | 8 | 9 | 9 | 10 | 10 | 11 | 12 | alt. rows. |

Cont. raglan shapings only until 2 sts. remain. K.2 tog. Fasten off.
Right front
As for left front, reversing the shapings, and noting that the k.2 togs. in the raglan shapings will be t.b.l.

V-necked cardigan

(See notes on buttonholes before commencing.)
Left front
As for button-to-the-neck cardigan to armhole. Discontinue buttonholes near this point.

With set-in sleeves only

Armhole
Cast off

| | 3 | 3 | 3 | 4 | 4 | 5 | 5 | 6 | 6 | 7 | 7 | 8 | 8 | 9 | 9 | sts. |

at armhole edge. K. to last 11 sts., k.2 tog., rib 9.
Next row: Rib 9, p. to end. Dec. 1 st. at armhole edge for next

| | 4 | 6 | 6 | 6 | 7 | 7 | 8 | 8 | 9 | 7 | 8 | 11 | 13 | 14 | 17 | alt. rows. |

Size	46	51	56	61	66	71	76	81	86	91	96	102	107	112	117	cm
	18	20	22	24	26	28	30	32	34	36	38	40	42	44	46	in.

At the same time dec. 1 st. at inside front border every 4th row until

| | 30 | 30 | 30 | 31 | 33 | 35 | 37 | 39 | 41 | 44 | 45 | 46 | 47 | 48 | 49 | sts. rem. |

Cont. straight until armhole matches back armhole.

Shape shoulder
Cast off

| | 7 | 7 | 7 | 7 | 8 | 9 | 9 | 10 | 11 | 12 | 12 | 12 | 13 | 13 | 13 | sts. |

at shoulder edge of next 2 alt. rows, then rem.

| | 7 | 7 | 7 | 8 | 8 | 8 | 10 | 10 | 10 | 11 | 12 | 13 | 12 | 13 | 14 | sts. |

Cont. on 9 border sts. only until work is sufficiently long to reach half-way across back neck. Cast off.

Right front
As for left front, reversing the shapings.

With raglan sleeves only
Armhole & raglan shapings
Cast off

| | 2 | 2 | 2 | 3 | 4 | 5 | 6 | 7 | 8 | 9 | 10 | 10 | 10 | 10 | 10 | sts. |

at armhole edge, k. to last 9 sts., rib 9.
Next row: Rib 9, p. to end.
1st row: K.3, k.2 tog., k. to last 11 sts., k.2 tog., rib 9.
2nd row: Rib 9, p. to end.
3rd row: K. to last 9 sts., rib 9.
4th row: Rib 9, p. to end.
Commence dec. 1 st. at neck edge in every 4th row, and rept. the above 4 rows twice. Then rept. 1st and 2nd rows only until the 9 border sts. remain. Continue on these 9 sts. until the work is sufficiently long to reach half-way across back neck. Cast off.
Right front
As for left front,

Size	46 18	51 20	56 22	61 24	66 26	71 28	76 30	81 32	86 34	91 36	96 38	102 40	107 42	112 44	117 46	cm in.

reversing the shapings,
and noting that the
k.2 togs. will be t.b.l.

Lumberjacket

Left front
Using 3¼ mm needles,
cast on — 41, 45, 49, 53, 57, 61, 65, 69, 73, 77, 81, 85, 89 sts.
Rib for — 8, 8, 10, 10, 12, 12, 14, 14, 16, 16, 18, 18, 18 rows.

Change to 4 mm
needles.
Cont. straight until work
measures — 23, 25.5, 28, 30.5, 33, 35, 35, 37, 38, 39.5, 39.5, 40.5, 40.5 cm
9, 10, 11, 12, 13, 13½, 14, 14½, 15, 15½, 15½, 16, 16 in.

With set-in sleeve tops only
Armholes
Cast off — 3, 4, 4, 5, 5, 6, 6, 7, 7, 8, 8, 9, 9 sts.
at armhole edge, then
dec. 1 st. at armhole
edge until — 33, 35, 38, 42, 44, 47, 50, 55, 57, 59, 60, 62, 65 sts. rem.

Cont. straight until
armhole measures (on
straight) — 6.5, 6.5, 7, 7.5, 8, 9, 9, 9.5, 10, 11.5, 11.5, 12.5, 15 cm
2½, 2½, 2¾, 3, 3¼, 3½, 3½, 3¾, 4, 4½, 4½, 5, 6 in.

less than back armhole,
when measured down
from the highest
shoulder point.
At neck edge
Cast off — 8, 8, 9, 9, 9, 9, 10, 11, 12, 12, 12, 12, 13 sts.
and dec. 1 st. at neck
edge on foll. — 4, 5, 5, 7, 6, 8, 8, 9, 9, 10, 10, 11, 12 alt. rows.

Cont. straight until
armhole measures the
same as the back
armhole.
Shape shoulder
Cast off — 7, 7, 8, 9, 9, 10, 11, 12, 12, 12, 13, 13, 13 sts.

at shoulder edge of next
2 alt. rows, and then
remaining — 7, 8, 8, 8, 10, 10, 10, 11, 12, 13, 12, 13, 14 sts.
Right front
As for left front,
reversing the shapings.

With raglan sleeve tops only

Armholes & raglan shaping

Size	46 / 18	51 / 20	56 / 22	61 / 24	66 / 26	71 / 28	76 / 30	81 / 32	86 / 34	91 / 36	96 / 38	102 / 40	107 / 42	112 / 44	117 / 46	

Cast off

| | | | 2 | 3 | 4 | 5 | 6 | 7 | 8 | 9 | 10 | 10 | 10 | 10 | 10 | sts. |

at armhole edge, k. to end.

Next row: P.

1st row: K.3, k.2 tog., k. to end.

2nd row: P.

3rd row: K.

4th row: P.

Rept. these 4 rows twice, then 1st and 2nd rows only until armhole measures

| | | | 6.5 | 6.5 | 7 | 7.5 | 8 | 9 | 9 | 9.5 | 10 | 11.5 | 11.5 | 12.5 | 15 | cm |
| | | | 2½ | 2½ | 2¾ | 3 | 3¼ | 3½ | 3½ | 3¾ | 4 | 4½ | 4½ | 5 | 6 | in. |

less than back armhole, when measuring down from the highest shoulder point.

At neck edge

Cast off

| | | | 8 | 8 | 9 | 9 | 9 | 9 | 10 | 11 | 12 | 12 | 12 | 12 | 13 | sts. |

and, continuing the raglan shapings, dec. 1 st. at neck-edge on foll.

| | | | 4 | 5 | 5 | 7 | 6 | 8 | 8 | 9 | 9 | 10 | 10 | 11 | 12 | alt. rows. |

Cont. raglan shapings only until 2 sts. remain. K.2 tog. Fasten off.

Right front

As for left front, reversing the shapings and noting that the k.2 togs. in the raglan shapings will be t.b.l.

Sleeves

Long sleeves

(Both alike)

Using 2¾ mm needles, cast on

| | 45 | 47 | 49 | 51 | 53 | 55 | 57 | 59 | 61 | 63 | 65 | 67 | 69 | 71 | 73 | sts. |

Rib for

| | 8 | 8 | 8 | 8 | 10 | 10 | 12 | 12 | 14 | 14 | 16 | 16 | 18 | 18 | 18 | rows. |

Change to 3¼ mm needles.

Work 10 rows.

Inc. 1 st. each end of next and every foll. 8th row until there are

| | 65 | 67 | 69 | 69 | 75 | 81 | 85 | 91 | 95 | 99 | 103 | 107 | 111 | 115 | 119 | sts. |

Cont. straight until sleeve edge measures

| | 20 | 21.5 | 23 | 25.5 | 30.5 | 33 | 35.5 | 38 | 40.5 | 43 | 46 | 48.25 | 48.25 | 48.25 | 48.25 | cm |
| | 8 | 8½ | 9 | 10 | 11 | 13 | 14 | 15 | 16 | 17 | 18 | 19 | 19 | 19 | 19 | in. |

or length required.

Size	46	51	56	61	66	71	76	81	86	91	96	102	107	112	117	cm
	18	20	22	24	26	28	30	32	34	36	38	40	42	44	46	in.

With set-in sleeve tops only

Cast off
at beg. next 2 rows. — 3, 3, 3, 4, 4, 5, 5, 6, 6, 7, 7, 8, 8, 9, 9 sts.

	46	51	56	61	66	71	76	81	86	91	96	102	107	112	117	
Cast off at beg. next 2 rows.	3	3	3	4	4	5	5	6	6	7	7	8	8	9	9	sts.

Dec. 1 st. at each end of
next 6 rows. Work
1 row without shaping.
1st row: Dec. 1 st. at
each end.
2nd row: Dec. 1 st. at
each end.
3rd row: Work without
shaping.

Rept. these 3 rows until	23	25	27	29	31	35	35	37	39	39	41	41	43	43	45	sts. rem.
Dec. 1 st. at each end of next Cast off.	4	5	5	6	6	6	6	8	8	9	9	10	10	11	11	rows.

With raglan sleeve tops only

Cast off at beg. next 2 rows, then:	2	2	2	3	4	5	6	7	8	9	10	10	10	10	10	sts.

1st row: K.3, k.2 tog., k.
to last 5 sts., k.2 t.b.l.,
k.3.
2nd row: P.
3rd row: K.
4th row: P.
Rept. these 4 rows
twice, then 1st and 2nd

rows only until	7	7	7	7	7	7	7	7	9	9	9	9	9	9	9	sts. rem.

Cast off.

Short sleeves

(Both alike)
If the recipient has thin
upper arms, cast on
4 sts. less than the
instructions and work
the cuff, increasing 4 sts.
evenly across the last
cuff row.
Using 2¾ mm needles,

cast on	59	61	63	67	71	75	81	85	91	95	99	101	105	111	113	sts.
Rib for	8	8	8	8	10	10	12	12	14	14	16	16	18	18	18	rows.

Change to 3¼ mm
needles.

		Size	46	51	56	61	66	71	76	81	86	91	96	102	107	112	117	cm
			18	20	22	24	26	28	30	32	34	36	38	40	42	44	46	in.

Inc. 1 st. each end 1st
and every foll. 4th row

until there are	65	67	69	69	75	81	85	91	95	99	103	107	111	115	119	sts.

Cont. straight until

sleeve edge measures	6.5	6.5	6.5	6.5	6.5	7	7.5	7.5	9	9	10	13	13.5	14	15.25	cm.
	2½	2½	2½	2½	2½	2¾	3	3	3½	3½	4	5	5¼	5½	6	in.

With set-in sleeve tops only

As for set-in sleeve tops
of long-sleeve
instructions.

With raglan sleeve tops only

As for raglan sleeve
tops of long-sleeve
instructions.

Neckbands, collars and armbands

Crew, turtle and polo neckbands
With set-in sleeves only

Join one shoulder seam.
Open out.

With raglan sleeves only

Stitch sleeves to front
and back, leaving one
seam open. Open out.

All styles
Using 2¾ mm needles,

pick up and k.	80	88	94	101	109	119	123	129	133	135	137	139	141	143	145	sts.

evenly around the neck.

Crew neck only
Work 10 rows for a
single neckband. Cast off.
Work 20 rows for a
double neckband. Cast off.
Fold to inside and catch
loosely all around.
Turtle neck only
Work 30 rows. Cast off.
Fold to inside and catch
loosely all round.
Polo neck only
Work 10 cm (4 in.) for a
child's garment, 15 cm

Size	46	51	56	61	66	71	76	81	86	91	96	102	107	112	117	cm
	18	20	22	24	26	28	30	32	34	36	38	40	42	44	46	ins

(6 in.) for a lady's
garment and 18 cm
(7 in.) for a man's.
Fold in half to the
outside.

Round neckbands (for high-necked cardigans)

Using 2¾ mm needles, pick up and k.	95	99	103	107	111	115	121	125	129	133	137	141	145	149	153	sts.

evenly around the neck.
This figure includes the
border sts. from the two
safety-pins.
Work in rib, making a
buttonhole over 4th-5th
rows in an 8-row band,
or 5th-6th rows in a
10-row band.

	8	8	8	8	8	10	10	10	10	10	10	10	10	10	10	rows.

Collars (for lumberjackets & high-necked cardigans)

Using 2¾ mm needles, cast on	66	70	74	78	82	86	90	94	98	103	108	113	118	123	127	sts.

Rib for:
28 rows (child's garment)
32 rows (lady's garment)
38 rows (man's garment).
Cast off.

V-neckbands

With set-in sleeves only

Join right shoulder seam.

With raglan sleeves only

Stitch sleeve raglan
shapings to front and
back raglan shapings,
leaving one seam open.
Open out.

All styles
Using 2¾ mm needles, r.s.f., pick up and k.			111	121	129	137	145	153	161	169	173	179	189	193	197	sts.

including the st. from
the safety-pin. Mark this
st. with a coloured thread.
1st row: Rib until 2 sts.
before the centre
(marked) st., k.2 tog.
t.b.l., p.1, k.2 tog., rib to end.

Size	46	51	56	61	66	71	76	81	86	91	96	102	107	112	117	cm
	18	20	22	24	26	28	30	32	34	36	38	40	42	44	46	ins
2nd row: Rib until 2 sts. before the centre (marked) st., p.2 tog., k.1, p.2 tog. t.b.l., rib to end.																
Rept. these 2 rows			3	3	3	3	3	4	4	4	4	5	5	5	5 times.	
Cast off ribwise using 3¼ mm needles.																

Armbands (for sleeveless v-necked pullovers)

	46	51	56	61	66	71	76	81	86	91	96	102	107	112	117	
Stitch left shoulder seam and neckband. Using 2¾ mm needles, pick up and k. evenly around the armhole. Rib for			111	117	121	127	129	135	139	141	143	147	151	155	157	sts.
			8	8	8	8	8	10	10	10	10	12	12	12	12 rows.	
Cast off ribwise using 3¼ mm needles.																

Tank tops

Back

	46	51	56	61	66	71	76	81	86	91	96	102	107	112	117	
Using 2¾ mm needles, cast on			77	85	93	101	107	111	119	127	135	143				sts.
Rib for			7.5	7.5	7.5	10	10	10	10	10	10	10				cm
			3	3	3	4	4	4	4	4	4	4				in.
Change to 3¼ mm needles. Cont. straight until work measures			18	20	21.5	24	27	29	29	29	32	32				cm
			7	8	8½	9½	10½	11½	11½	11½	12½	12½				in.
Armholes Cast off at beg. of next 2 rows.			6	6	6	7	7	8	8	9	9	10				sts.
Dec. 1 st. at each end every row until			57	61	65	69	73	81	85	89	93	97				sts. rem.
Work straight until the armhole measures (on straight)			13	14	15	16	17	20	21	22	24	25				cm
			5	5½	6	6¼	6¾	8	8¼	8½	9½	9¾				in.
Shape shoulders Cast off at beg. of next 2 rows.			7	8	8	9	9	8	8	8	9	9				sts.

Size	46 / 18	51 / 20	56 / 22	61 / 24	66 / 26	71 / 28	76 / 30	81 / 32	86 / 34	91 / 36	96 / 38	102 / 40	107 / 42	112 / 44	117 / 46	cm / ins
Cast off at beg. of the foll. 2 rows.			8	8	9	9	10	8	8	8	9	9	sts.			
Sizes 81-101 cm (32-40 in.) only Cast off							7	8	9	8	9	sts.				
All sizes Cast off remaining			27	29	31	33	35	35	37	39	41	43	sts.			

Front

Work as for tank top back until the armhole shapings are complete and 57 / 61 / 65 / 69 / 73 / 81 / 85 / 89 / 93 / 97 sts. rem. (columns 56–102)

	46 / 18	51 / 20	56 / 22	61 / 24	66 / 26	71 / 28	76 / 30	81 / 32	86 / 34	91 / 36	96 / 38	102 / 40	107 / 42	112 / 44	117 / 46	cm / ins
and			57	61	65	69	73	81	85	89	93	97	sts. rem.			
Neck K.			18	19	20	22	23	26	28	30	32	33	sts.			
Cast off next			21	23	25	25	27	29	29	29	29	31	sts.			
K. to end. Working on last set of sts. only, dec. 1 st. at neck edge on every row until			15	16	17	18	19	23	24	25	26	27	sts. rem.			
Shape shoulder At shoulder edge cast off			7	8	8	9	9	8	8	8	9	9	sts.			
Next row: P. Cast off at beg. next row.			8	8	9	9	10	8	8	8	9	9	sts.			
Sizes 81-101 cm (32-40 in.) only *Next row:* P. Cast off remaining							7	8	9	8	9	sts.				

Join the wool at the centre front, and complete the other side front to match, reversing the shapings.

Neck and armhole bands

Neckbands
Stitch right shoulder seam. Using 2¾ mm needles, r.s.f., pick up and k. evenly around the neck.

	46 / 18	51 / 20	56 / 22	61 / 24	66 / 26	71 / 28	76 / 30	81 / 32	86 / 34	91 / 36	96 / 38	102 / 40	107 / 42	112 / 44	117 / 46	cm / ins
pick up and k.			130	138	146	154	164	172	178	186	210	216	sts.			

Rib for 10 rows. Cast off ribwise using 3¼ mm needles.

Size	46	51	56	61	66	71	76	81	86	91	96	102	107	112	117	cm
	18	20	22	24	26	28	30	32	34	36	38	40	42	44	46	ins

Armbands
Stitch left shoulder
seam and neckband.
Using 2¾ mm needles,
r.s.f., pick up and k.

			90	98	106	118	128	140	156	164	180	188	sts.

evenly around armhole.
Rib for

			8	8	8	8	8	10	10	10	10	12	rows.

Cast off ribwise using
3¼ mm needles.

To facilitate reading the charts set out details here for any patterns you intend to repeat often.

To facilitate reading the charts set out details here for any patterns you intend to repeat often.